FAST & THRIFTY WAYS
TO CLEAN EVERYTHING
IN YOUR HOME

VENTURA BOOKS
New York City
Printed in the United States
All Rights Reserved

FAST & THRIFTY WAYS TO CLEAN EVERYTHING IN YOUR HOME

TABLE OF CONTENTS

INTRODUCTION TO HELPFUL HINTS BOOK

What do you do when you're just about to give a big party and you notice that your parquet floors are scratched? Should you throw your broom away just because the bristles are too soft to do a good job any longer? What's the best way to clean your metal objects? How can you get gum out of your favorite rug or carpet? What can you do when your steam iron has brown spots on its bottom?

In order to keep your house in tip-top shape, it helps to have a repertoire of good household hints at your fingertips that will take the guess-work out of cleaning, and solve the traumas—large and small—that come with taking care of household possessions.

In this book, you will find the best of everything—hints that are designed to make your daily household chores run more smoothly than ever before. You'll also find some of the favorite ways to take care of your finer things or restore them to their former beauty if they have gotten stained or dirty. In short, this book will provide hints on the best care for everyday cleaning that will prevent major problems from setting in.

Of course, you can never avoid all of the major household mishaps—a child can write on your walls with crayons or you can suddenly run out of eyeglass cleaner, etc. But, if you take care of your house on a regular basis, using the special tips that are given in this book, you'll avoid the *unnecessary* problems. And there are many hints for the household emergencies, as well.

These hints fall into a variety of categories—some are just basic good care for every major area of your house and some are those touches that make everything run better and smoother. They have been collected over the years from a variety of sources— friends, relatives, and neighbors. Some have been handed down for generations, and others are new things that are the result of technology. They are all based on the premise that most people want to spend less time and money on their housework, and yet want their day-to-day housecleaning to be as easy as possible.

The book is divided into sections, so that you can find the hints you need easily. First is a chapter on the real basics—Cleaning Aids and Tools of the Trade. One chapter deals with the care of Laundry and Fabrics, Floors and Furniture comprise another. There is a special section for your Collectibles and Decorative Accessories, and another for Kitchen Appliances, Countertops and Cookware, and still another for Walls, Windows and Ceilings. Finally, there is a group of Miscellaneous hints. These don't fit into any specific category, but each and every one of them is a gem.

Not only is this book designed to save you time, but also to save you money. Last, but not least, this book is designed to give you great convenience. The hints and tips are arranged in an easy-to-read manner, so that it is very simple to find the subject you are looking for. By dividing the book into chapters, with a brief description of what sorts of hints are in each one, you should be able to locate a subject very quickly, if you need to find something fast. You'll find that these hints make your household day easier to get through, and they'll save you money, too.

Cleaning aids and TOOLS OF THE TRADE

INTRODUCTION FOR:
CLEANING AIDS AND TOOLS OF THE TRADE

In order to keep your house in the condition you want—clean and sparkling—you must first have the right tools. You can clean and scrub for hours, but if you're using the wrong cleaning solution or applicator, you'll get only a fraction of the results that you should, and much of your effort will be wasted.

CLEANING AIDS AND TOOLS OF THE TRADE provides you with concise and helpful information on a wide range of household cleaning jobs. In this chapter you will find ways to cut down on your cleaning budget and still get the best in quality cleaning agents, and tips on what tools are really necessary to keep around. There are hints on how to turn ordinary kitchen supplies, like cornstarch and vinegar into homemade solutions for almost any job, and special attention is devoted to hard-to-clean areas like the bathroom. You'll find money-saving tips on aerosol sprays and sound advice on dangerous products to avoid.

This chapter gives you all you need to know about the means to keeping your apartment or home spotless.

A TIP FOR AEROSOL USERS.
Although products for just about every chore in the house now come in aerosol form, cost-wise they are usually a very poor buy. You end up paying many times over the worth of the cleaner, and sometimes, because they are under pressure, the quality is inferior, too.

WHAT SHOULD BE USED INSTEAD OF AEROSOLS?
Buy a supply of reusable plastic spray bottles from your local hardware store, 5 & 10, or even an industrial cleaning supply place. Then get your cleaning supplies in concentrated form and dilute them according to the instructions for each one. Put the new solution into your plastic spray bottles—and presto! you'll have your very own supply of easy-to-use spray bottles. Not

only will you have a better product, but you'll be saving a lot of money, too.

CLEAN BETTER WITH LESS.
Is it true that if using 1/2 cup of ammonia to a certain amount of water is good, then a full cup will do twice as well? Absolutely not. Too much of any detergent or chemical in your cleaning water can actually destroy the action of the chemical. It is very important to read the directions very carefully in order to let the cleaning "helpers" do the job correctly for you.

IF YOUR FAVORITE CANE SEAT HAS BEGUN TO LOOSEN, HERE'S AN EASY WAY TO RESTORE IT.
Water will do the trick! Just wet the cane down and then let it dry. The cane will be nice and taut once again.

DON'T CONFUSE RUSH WITH CANE.
There is a big difference between rush and cane, so don't make the mistake of cleaning them in the same fashion. Cane responds beautifully to water, but rush does not. If you try to wet rush, you will damage the rush fibers and your rush chair may be ruined. So heed this warning.

IF YOU'VE JUST CLEANED YOUR SLIPCOVERS, REMEMBER THIS TIP TO GET THEM BACK ON SMOOTHLY.
Slipcovers, if they are well made, look like a "second skin" for your furniture. So in order to get your slipcover looking nice and taut when it is back on the furniture after a washing, don't wait until it dries completely. A slipcover should be replaced while it is still a bit damp, for then it will dry into place beautifully.

IF YOU LOVE YOUR ROCKING CHAIR, BUT IT IS SCRATCHING AND DAMAGING YOUR FINE FLOOR, HERE'S HELP.
Simply take a piece of soft fabric—heavy velvet or felt will do—and cut two strips to fit the bottom of the rocker. Apply with some liquid glue, turn the rocker upside down to dry

thoroughly, and you'll be able to rock away with no harm to your floor.

GET A WAX APPLICATOR JUST FOR YOUR FLOORS— IT PAYS DIVIDENDS.

For cleaning your floors, an applicator that is fitted with a lamb's wool pad is well worth the purchase. It should be used only for your floors. It spreads wax evenly and allows your floors to shine.

A MULTI-PURPOSE CLEANER WILL GO A LONG WAY.

A good multi-purpose cleaner which is free of phosphate can be purchased at your local hardware store. You can also find this product in larger quantities in an industrial cleaning supply company. This cleaner will dissolve quickly and do a first-rate cleaning job. But one warning—use rubber or plastic gloves if this product is used, to protect your hands.

CAREFUL! NOT EVERYTHING CAN BE WASHED.

One product that you will need if there is any wallpaper in your home is a special cleaner. Ask your local hardware store for something that is designed just for your wallpaper. This is a product similar to clay which you stroke to absorb any dirt. It will prevent your wallpaper from losing its bright color, since water may tend to dull the colors of your wall covering.

KEEP AN ART ERASER HANDY FOR TOUGH PENCIL MARKERS.

A relatively inexpensive tool which you cannot afford to be without is an eraser of the ordinary art-store variety. This can be used to remove any dirty smudges from the wall surface.

IS LEMON OIL MADE FROM LEMONS A GOOD WOOD POLISH?

Paraffin oil forms the basis of so-called lemon oil, and the lemon is only for cosmetic purposes. So, don't think that you are getting a lemon product. It does help to keep the wood from drying out by soaking into the furniture, but only on furniture which is not varnished or shellacked. Once there is a coating, the oil cannot penetrate.

WHEN YOU USE LEMON OIL, HERE'S A HINT THAT WILL HELP IT WORK AT ITS BEST.

Lemon oil can build up with usage over a period of time. In order to make it work at its best, remove the lemon oil before you apply the next coat. This will help it to work better.

HERE'S A WAY TO KEEP THE SOIL AWAY FROM YOUR CARPETING OR UPHOLSTERY. KEEP IT AMONG YOUR CLEANING SUPPLIES.

"Scotchgard" is a product which is specifically designed to slow down the process of dirt seeping into your rugs or upholstered pieces. In addition, it has a protective coating which prevents dirt and liquid stains from penetrating your fine upholstery.

TO CUT DOWN ON YOUR CLEANING SUPPLY BUDGET AND GET THE BEST IN QUALITY, FIND YOUR JANI-TORIAL SUPPLY HOUSE.

This is the best way to get good buys and the best in cleaning supplies. By using professional cleaning equipment, you'll be able to save lots of time and money. Although some of these concentrated cleaning supplies may APPEAR to be more expensive, they dilute and are actually cost-saving.

SOMETIMES ORDINARY CORNSTARCH CAN DO WONDERS!

If you have greasy spots that are not responding to your regular cleaning methods, try blotting the spot with a regular desk blotter, or even some heavy paper towels. Then, sprinkle a bit of cornstarch on the offensive spot, and allow it to seep in. It will absorb the grease and then you can gently rub the spot off.

ALWAYS KEEP AN OLD TOOTHBRUSH HANDY FOR HOUSECLEANING.

When your old toothbrush has outlived its usefulness, retire it into your cleaning tool supply. It will come in very handy for those hard-to-reach corners.

RENT PROFESSIONAL EQUIPMENT FOR CLEANING HEAVILY SOILED CARPETING.

Sometimes, despite your best efforts, your floors or carpets can get beyond the point where ordinary methods work. Most hardware or paint stores carry a line of heavy-duty industrial equipment which is available at a very reasonable rate for rental. One of these is a steam machine for cleaning carpets which has a beater. This is a heavy-duty cleaner that will loosen the dirt in the carpet while the water is still present. Sometimes you may even be able to find it at your local grocery store.

IF YOU'RE TEMPTED TO USE KEROSENE FOR YOUR CLEANING, TAKE THIS WORD OF WARNING.

Although kerosene is a solvent, it is also an oil, and will leave a coat of oil on whatever you treat with it. In addition, it really has a very foul odor, which is sure to linger for hours.

HERE'S A HINT IF YOU NEED TO REMOVE OILY STAINS.

Rather than the use of kerosene, try some dry-cleaning fluid, or even some of the thinner that you use when you paint.

IF YOU ARE TEMPTED TO USE LINSEED OIL TO POLISH YOUR WOOD SURFACES, HEED THIS WARNING. IT WON'T WORK.

Linseed oil is not designed to polish a wood finish on your fine wood surfaces, because it just does not penetrate the varnish. It is designed for unfinished wood, so save your money and prevent your wood furniture from getting the tacky surface that comes from the improper use of linseed oil.

ALWAYS KEEP SOME STEEL WOOL IN SEVERAL GRADES HANDY. IT CAN WORK WONDERS.

There are many uses for steel wool. This is a product that you should keep on hand for your cleaning needs. Keep several grades, from coarse to very fine, at hand. You can use it to remove caked-on dirt. This works for particularly "dirty" jobs like the chimney grate. But be cautious—it's not good for items such as ceramic glazed tile.

AMMONIA CAN BE ONE OF YOUR BEST FRIENDS WHEN YOU CLEAN.

Ammonia can be considered one of the miracle products in your household. Often, it can be mixed with other substances to form an effective and inexpensive cleaner. However, be careful about how you use it. You must always work in an area where the ventilation is good, and never use more ammonia than is called for.

A GOOD WAX REMOVER WILL MAKE YOUR LIFE SIMPLER WHEN CLEANING FLOORS.

In order to avoid that yellowed look on your waxed floors, use a floor remover to take away that built-up wax. There are products made to make this chore easier, for they strip away all of the wax and allow you to start all over again.

NEVER MAKE THE MISTAKE OF THINKING THAT A GOOD THICK COAT WILL REPLACE TWO THIN ONES.

It can be very tempting to assume that if directions on a cleaner call for two thin coats, that one thick one will do the job even better. Not true. Often using one coat instead of two will make your application thick and gloppy. There's a good reason for directions being given the way they are. Follow them.

HERE'S AN ECONOMICAL WAY TO CLEAN YOUR FABRIC UPHOLSTERY.

Take a mild liquid dishwashing detergent. Mix a solution of 2 cups of lukewarm water and add 1/3 of a cup of the liquid detergent. Then put the solution in your blender and mix until foamy. This will do the cleaning job beautifully.

DON'T LET YOUR LAMP SCRATCH YOUR GOOD WOOD FURNITURE.

It is very easy to ensure that your wood furniture stays in fine condition if you take some precautions. Cut a pad of felt or some other soft fabric to fit the shape of the bottom of your lamp base. Apply with some liquid glue, and you'll never have to worry about unsightly scratches again.

IF YOU ARE GOING TO VACUUM YOUR FURNITURE, DO IT THOROUGHLY.

Don't be tempted to vacuum your fine furniture on the surface only. Take all of the cushions that are removeable off the sofa or chair and vacuum the crevices with the special attachment of your vacuum cleaner. Then vacuum each cushion thoroughly and return to place.

FOLLOW THE WOOD GRAIN FOR BEST RESULTS.

Every natural wood has a grain. It is important to determine which direction the grain runs, because if you polish your wood in the direction of the grain, you will really bring that shine up to its absolute best.

HERE'S A SOLUTION THAT IS INEXPENSIVE TO MAKE, AND WILL WORK WONDERS FOR YOUR CERAMIC TILE.

Use a mixture of 1 cup of vinegar, 3/4 cups of ammonia and about 1/4 cup of baking soda. Add these to 1 gallon of luke-warm water. Now, this will be a very strong brew, and so we recommend that you use the solution carefully. If you store it, be sure it is well covered. Then use protective gloves when working with it. Always be sure that you rinse thoroughly with warm water and wipe dry.

IF YOUR BATHROOM TILE LOOKS DIRTY AND DULL, GO THE PROFESSIONAL ROUTE!

The professionals really know what they're doing. For use in kitchens or bathrooms that have tiled areas, use industrial strength bathroom cleaner. This is especially formulated for those tough jobs.

WHENEVER YOU USE PRODUCTS THAT DO A GREAT CLEANING JOB, HEED THIS.

Usually when you use very strong products, they are designed to do a super cleaning job. But, often they leave residue film that should be cleaned off with clear water. So be sure that you check the directions carefully and if they call for a rinse, do not skip this essential step.

IF YOUR BATHROOM TILE HAS ACCUMULATED MILDEW, TREAT IT SPECIALLY.

There are products made especially for removing mildew stains from tile grouting. You can usually find these at your local hardware store, but be sure to use it only for that purpose.

WHAT KINDS OF SPONGES WORK BEST FOR CLEANING JOBS?

Two basic sponges will do the trick. A dry sponge, which is made of natural rubber that has been chemically treated, does a neat job on walls and ceilings, and a double-layer nylon sponge should be used when you need a wet sponge. You can find both at your local hardware store or Five & Ten.

WHAT KIND OF CLEANING CLOTHS ARE NEEDED?

A terry cloth large enough to be doubled over is a must. This can be used for many different types of cleaning surfaces, including ceilings or walls. Another good cloth is one that is treated to keep the dust in place rather than allowing it to fly all around—that is called Masslin cloth. They can be bought almost anywhere.

WHAT ABOUT CLEANERS? HOW MANY ARE NEEDED?

Only two basic types—a concentrated neutral cleaner, to be used for all cleaning where you don't need a disinfectant, and a concentrated disinfectant cleaner where you need to sanitize the area.

HERE'S HOW TO REACH HIGH ENOUGH TO CLEAN THOSE HARD-TO-GET PLACES:

Get an extension handle, which comes so that it can extend up to 8 feet when attached to brushes or squeegees, and that will help you safely reach those spots normally out of reach.

HERE'S THE BEST WAY TO DUST VERY HIGH PLACES, LIKE THE TOPS OF PICTURE FRAMES OR MOLDINGS:

The best cleaning implement is a duster made of synthetic lamb's wool, and the ideal handle length is between 22" and 24".

DON'T RUIN YOUR SQUEEGEE.

The squeegee should be used *only* for cleaning your windows, because other uses will dull the blade.

A FEATHER DUSTER IS PRETTY...

but a feather duster just moves the dust from one place to another. Treated Masslin cloths are truly the best.

PREVENT YOUR CLEANING CLOTH FROM SNAGGING ON THE TOPS OF DOORS OR SHELVES!

Here's a tip for a common complaint. Often, those hard-to-reach places are unfinished, and so your best bet is to smooth them with sandpaper, and then use some paint or varnish to match the surface.

WINDOW SILLS COLLECT SO MUCH DUST. NO MATTER HOW MUCH YOU DUST THEM, THEY NEVER SEEM TO BE DUST-FREE. HERE'S A GREAT HINT.

The simplest and most effective way to clean dust from window sills is a cloth that has been slightly dampened with some clear water. This way, you'll simply pick the dust up, and won't leave any tell-tale greasy film behind.

WATCH THAT BLEACH.

Bleach is a whitening agent, NOT a cleaner. Because we think of it as being so strong, it seems as if it should be used for everything. But it doesn't really clean that well, and can even be dangerous. Even properly diluted chlorine bleach can cause damage to your upholstery and plastic surfaces. Plus any sudden splashing on furniture or even on the cleaner can be quite dangerous. Keep it in the laundry room, away from children, where it belongs.

WHAT ABOUT ADDING SOME BLEACH TO YOUR BOWL CLEANER TO MAKE YOUR BATHROOM SUPER SPOTLESS?

Not unless you want to be exposed to the vapors of chlorine gas, which is extremely dangerous. NEVER mix bleach with any of the commercial bowl cleaners.

HERE'S A TIP THAT WILL CUT DOWN ON THE MAJORITY OF YOUR HOUSECLEANING BEFORE IT EVEN BEGINS. IT'S SO GOOD THAT WE CONSIDER THE SIMPLE MAT A HOUSECLEANING TOOL!

If you place a mat inside your entry door, and outside too, you'll eliminate a major source of home dirt before it has a chance to settle into your valuable carpets or furniture. Just place a mat about 2-1/2 to 3-1/2 feet by 3-1/2 to 5 feet outside and inside your front door. Then you can clean the mat daily and your work will be cut down drastically.

LAUNDRY and FABRICS

INTRODUCTION FOR LAUNDRY

Doing laundry chores can often be tedious and time-consuming, and we all know how dry cleaning costs have quadrupled in the past few years. To help you deal with laundry needs in a more efficient and money-saving way, we have provided this chapter of helpful hints.

Designed to remove the guess-work out of doing laundry, and free your valuable time for doing more enjoyable tasks, this group of hints forms one of the most basic chapters in this book. Read it and you'll discover how to clean everything from the proper care of pillows, to leather gloves, down coats, and woolen sweaters. We tell you the best and easiest way to remove perspiration, ink, grease, rust, coffee, alcohol, and blood stains, even how to get out those "impossible" stains—gum and tar.

Different fabrics require different care, and you should always carefully read labels and follow manufacturers' instructions. You also need a working knowledge of fabrics in general and the best way to clean and preserve them. We give you just that. We not only cover how to care for fine linens and lace, but also how to deal with doubly-soiled children's wear. We tell you what to do for outstretched knit cuffs and how to prevent hosiery from running.

You'll find ways to remove electricity cling from garments, tips on how to block material, and advice on how to avoid shrinkage. We offer suggestions on virtually every fabric from 100% cotton to nylon and acetate, plus tips on when to use and when not to use bleach, how to perk up old hats and what to do for leather belts. This chapter is an absolute must for everyone!

BUT, WHAT ABOUT LEATHER GLOVES? CAN THEY BE WASHED?
Well, the astounding answer, is "yes". After all, cows get wet, don't they? Simply do this: when washing leather gloves, do it while wearing them! Just put them on, and wash your "hands" with a mild soap. Wearing the gloves the gloves allows them to

retain their shape. Remember not to rub excessively, and lay the gloves flat to dry, away from any direct source of heat.

HERE'S A GREAT TIP FOR THE NEXT TIME YOU HAND-WASH YOUR SWEATERS.
Trace the outline of the sweater on piece of heavy tracing paper, in indelible marker. That way you'll have a guide when reblocking the sweater after washing.

And remember, never hang a hand-knit sweater on a hanger to dry. Lay it flat, or it'll be down to your knees the next time you take it out to wear it!

SOME TIPS ON HAND-WASHING:
Always hand-wash any garment gently, particularly knitted ones. Allow the suds to squeeze through the fabric rather than twisting or kneading it.

Always wash sweaters inside out to prevent any pilling.

Vinegar in the rinse water will alleviate all suds.

FABRICS

IN ORDER TO KEEP YOUR FIBERGLASS CURTAINS IN TOP CONDITION, BE SURE TO VACUUM THEM FREQUENTLY.
Rather than allow your fiberglass curtains to collect dust week after week, it is best to vacuum them from time to time. If you use the same attachment as you would for your sofa, you can whisk down the curtains quite quickly, and prevent unnecessary washing.

IT IS EASY TO WASH YOUR FIBERGLASS CURTAINS WHEN YOU PROTECT YOUR HANDS.
One of the problems with fiberglass is that there are small particles of actual glass in the fabric. Thus, when you are rub-

bing them, you run the risk of injuring your hands. To make the job easier, wear the rubber gloves that you use for heavy duty house cleaning whenever you handle these curtains.

IF YOU DO DECIDE TO USE YOUR WASHING MACHINE FOR YOUR FIBERGLASS CURTAINS, BE SURE TO PRE-SET THE CYCLE SO THAT YOU DO NOT USE THE SPIN CYCLE.

Fiberglass is particularly poor in resisting abrasion, although this fabric is also very slow to get dirty or wrinkled. However, if washed in a machine, you should avoid the spin cycles, which tend to destroy the fibers.

WHEN YOU WASH YOUR FIBERGLASS CURTAINS, BE SURE NOT TO WASH ANY GARMENTS AT THE SAME TIME.

Since there are particles of glass fiber present in fiberglass, it is best never to wash in the same load as any clothing. Thus, you can be sure to avoid the glass fibers penetrating your garments.

DOG DO-DO ON THE RUG?

That new puppy may be cute, but is probably driving you crazy while you train him or her. Not to mention that the little bugger is ruining your new carpet. Well, here's a step by step solution to your problem. Immediately remove all solids and use a soft paper towel to blot up any moisture. Then, spray the immediate area with shaving cream (yes, you heard right, *shaving cream*!). Allow the shaving cream to seep into the stained area for about 4 to 7 minutes. Next, gently sponge the area clean of foam and pour on a small amount of club soda. Let the soda fizz up before wiping it off, and then sponge clean with clear, cool water.

PERSPIRATION STAINS CAN REALLY RUIN YOUR WHITE CLOTHING.

Well, fight back. Problem perspiration can really ruin the appearance of some of your favorite white clothing with unsightly rings or stains. Just sponge on a mild solution of two parts spring water to one part white vinegar and then launder as usual. Presto! Your stain will be gone.

PRESOAKS MAY BE THE SOLUTION FOR DINGY CLOTHES.

With most presoaks that are on the market, you can leave clothes that have become dull and dingy soaking overnight. Just make sure the clothing is colorfast and soak away! Your clothes will look like new again in no time.

DO YOU HAVE SOME LACE PANTIES OR EVEN A BLOUSE THAT IS SIMPLY TOO DELICATE TO WITHSTAND EVEN THE MILDEST CYCLE ON YOUR WASHER? THIS SHOULD HELP.

You can wash even your most precious items by filling a container with some warm water, and then adding a bit of the mildest liquid soap you can find. Shake this solution until it is well blended, and then add your lace clothing. Shake thoroughly, and then allow the garments to soak for about a half hour. Rinse thoroughly in clear, warm water, but do not wring them out very much—just enough to get the bulk of water out. Then hang to dry, and you'll keep your fine lace garments in mint condition.

TRY THIS EASY HINT IF YOUR CHILD'S JEANS HAVE BECOME MUDDY—IT WILL WORK MAGIC!

First, run some cold, clear water into your bathtub and whisk the jeans through the water to get out the surface dirt. Then, fill the bathroom sink with a mixture of equal parts of a laundry detergent and household ammonia. Allow the jeans to soak for approximately six hours, then put through the regular wash cycle. The jeans should be free of mud.

IF YOUR FAVORITE SWEATER HAS STRETCHED-OUT CUFFS, HERE'S A WAY TO GET THEM BACK TO THEIR ORIGINAL SIZE.

Fill a basin with some hot water, and dip the cuffs into the water, allowing them to be thoroughly saturated. Then take your hand-held hair dryer, turn up to the "high" position, and carefully dry the cuffs, holding the dryer *no closer than* three inches from the sweater. The cuffs should resume their original shape.

25

SOAKING IS IMPORTANT IN HAND-WASHING.

Soaking garments too long in hand-washing soaps is hard on the fibers of the item. Instead, be sure to soak them only three to five minutes.

DON'T FORGET THE TEMPERATURE OF THE WATER.

Never hand-wash in hot water. Instead, hand laundering should be done in cold, or cool (luke-warm) water. And remember to always rinse them in cold water, too.

TO PREVENT EXCESSIVE WRINKLING...

Always remove your clothes from the dryer as soon as it stops. Shake out the clothing and hang it up as soon as possible. This will cut down on the amount of ironing necessary, and if you feel the same way about ironing as we do, we're sure you'll be glad to hear that one!

ARE YOUR CLOTHESPINS OLD, DIRTY, OR GRUNGEY LOOKING?

Well, clothespins get dirty, too. If they are plastic, simply put them in an open mesh laundry bag and throw them in the washing machine on "gentle" cycle, and they'll look new in no time. If they are the wonderfully old-fashioned, wooden kind, wash then in your sink in hot water and a strong solution of dishwashing detergent. Let them dry out of the (direct) sunlight, in a warm, well-ventilated place.

DO YOUR PANTY HOSE RUN WITHIN MINUTES OF THE TIME YOU PUT THEM ON? HERE'S A WAY TO PREVENT THIS PROBLEM.

Take some ordinary household spray starch—the kind that you spray on during the ironing process—and put a thin covering over your new panty hose. This should retard the process of "runs"—and it's best to do this even *before* you've worn them for the first time.

IF YOU ARE GETTING READY TO GO OUT TO AN IMPORTANT APPOINTMENT, AND SUDDENLY NOTICE

THAT YOUR WHITE BLOUSE HAS A STAIN, TRY THIS QUICK SOLUTION.

A temporary solution would be to take some ordinary talcum powder—and apply it to the spot on your blouse with an ordinary household cotton swab. By rubbing gently, you should be able to cover the offensive stain so that no-one will even notice.

IF YOUR CLOTHING HAS BEEN FOLDED INSIDE A SUITCASE AND HAS GOTTEN CREASED, A SIMPLE HOUSEHOLD SUPPLY CAN REMEDY THIS SITUATION.

Take a presscloth and saturate it with some white vinegar. Ring out thoroughly, so that it is just damp. Then use your iron—be sure it's not too hot—and the creases should disappear.

IF YOU LOVE OUTDOOR SPORTS SUCH AS SKATING OR WALKING IN THE SNOW, BUT DON'T WANT TO USE EXPENSIVE SPECIALTY CLOTHING, TRY THIS TRICK.

Take a pair of heavy slacks, or you can even use some old jeans. Spray them with a waterproof fabric spray, such as you would use for protecting a sofa. You'll be able to be in the snow to your heart's content without getting soaked through and through.

HERE'S A QUICK TIP ABOUT IRONING.

If you are going to iron the clothing that you take out of the dryer, *don't* let it dry completely. That little bit of moisture allows the fabric to wrinkle less and iron easier and smoother.

ABOUT YOUR DRYER...

Always remember to clean the lint filter after each use of the dryer. It cuts down strain on the machine and allows the machine to function at it's fullest, both performance-wise and economically.

HERE'S ANOTHER QUICK TIP FOR LAUNDRY DAY.

Save all the care tags and special instruction stickers from your clothing and tape or glue them in a loose-leaf or spiral-bound note book; you know, the kind you buy the kids for back to school. Also jot down notes on any hard-to-care-for items, and then keep the log book in the laundry. On wash day, consult the book when you need to.

DID YOU KNOW...
Many stains can be eradicated if they are "attacked" in time. For instance, many household products can be used as absorbant agents on a stain, spot or spill, and save you hours of frustrating work, trying to erase the stain later. They are: Corn starch, oatmeal, talcom powder and salt.

IF YOUR CANVAS ITEMS, SUCH AS POCKETBOOKS OR SHOES HAVE STARTED TO LOOK DINGY, HERE'S A WAY TO GET THEM AS GOOD AS NEW.
Take a brush—the kind you usually use to polish your regular shoes—and apply some rug shampoo to the canvas. You should be careful to brush gently, so that you don't disrupt the nap on the shoe.

IF YOUR WHITE SNEAKERS HAVE A TENDENCY TO GET GREY AND GRIMY, TRY THIS TO KEEP THEM LOOKING NEW FOR A LONGER TIME.
First, place the sneakers on several sheets of newspaper. Then, spray them evenly with some spray starch. You should use a regular spraying motion, and keep the spray flowing evenly onto the sneakers. This should maintain a longer lifetime for your favorite sports shoes.

WHEN YOUR FAVORITE BRAND OF PANTY HOSE IS UNAVAILABLE, AND YOU HAVE TO SUBSTITUTE, BUT FIND THE NEW PAIR HAS GONE OUT OF SHAPE, TRY THIS.
Take a bowl filled with some tepid water, and add a few table-spoons of regular household vinegar. Then soak the panty hose in this solution for approximately 15 minutes. Rinse in clear water, and your panty hose will be back in shape in no time.

IF YOU'RE DOWN TO YOUR LAST PAIR OF PANTY HOSE, BUT THEY ARE DIRTY AND YOU HAVE TO BE OUT OF THE HOUSE IN A SHORT TIME, THIS SOLUTION SHOULD WORK.

Wash the panty hose in warm water, then wring out well. Hang them on a hanger over your shower rod and place a towel underneath them to catch the excess moisture. Then, take your favorite hair blower, turn it on the low setting, and simply blow-dry your panty hose. Within several minutes, you'll have dry panty hose in time enough to zip out of the house!

WHAT ABOUT WASHING BEDSPREADS?

Quite simply, try it! Just dip a corner of the spread into a solution of your favorite detergent and warm water. If the colors remain fast, you can wash it. If they begin to run, have the bedspread drycleaned. Better safe than sorry.

IF YOUR BEDSPREAD IS WASHABLE...

When you dry it, remember to dry it alone on low heat in your dryer, with a few clean towels and a tennis shoe (clean, of course) to keep it company.

CAN WOOL BLANKETS BE WASHED BY MACHINE?

Most of them, yes. However, use a cold wash setting and a product like machine wash wool-lite to wash them in. And never, never dry them in your dryer.

BY USING SOME ORDINARY VINEGAR, YOU CAN KEEP YOUR SWEATERS FREE FROM THE ANNOYING SOAP FILM THAT OFTEN STAYS ON AFTER WASHING.

To ensure removing all of the soap which you have used in washing your favorite sweaters, just add about one-third cup of ordinary household vinegar to some tepid water. Immerse your sweater in this solution after you have washed it and rinsed it thoroughly. Then dunk up and down several times and wring out carefully. Be sure not to twist the sweater. You'll have a sweater free of soap, with the color back to its original vibrancy.

TRY THIS EASY WAY TO BLOCK YOUR SWEATERS AFTER THEY'VE BEEN WASHED.

To block your sweater, get a piece of window screen that has been framed in metal or wood. Place the sweater flat on the screen surface, and trace around the outline of your sweater with an indelible art marker. Be sure that the sweater is held firmly in place and does not move during this process. Then, wash your sweater, and block it back to its original shape by fitting it into the marker area on the screen. You can aid in faster drying by hanging the screen from a ceiling plant hook, preferably near a window, to allow the air to circulate on all sides.

IF YOU'VE GOTTEN INK ON YOUR FAVORITE LEATHER VEST OR SKIRT, TRY THIS EASY WAY TO REMOVE THE STAIN.

Get some ordinary baking soda, and apply it to the spot, rubbing gently with a clean piece of cloth. The baking powder will soak up the stain gradually. Keep using a fresh spot on the cloth and apply the baking soda several times. You will see the stain melt away in stages until it is all gone.

SORTING OUT THE DO'S AND DON'TS OF LAUNDRY.

Sorting is one of the essential things to remember about laundry. Pre-sorting cuts down wash time, eliminates ruined clothing (such as denim-blue undies) and your work load. Have three large containers or baskets, and make your household members each responsible for sorting their own laundry. One for whites and colorfast items, one for darks, and one for hand-wash.

REMEMBER THE CUFFS.

Remember to turn down cuffs, roll down sleeves and check through pockets before laundering anything. After all, there is nothing worse than washing Susie's bubblegum, Harold's paycheck, or Boby's pet bullfrog!

TEARS, RIPS AND HOLES.

Remember to mend all damaged clothing before laundering. Tears, rips and holes will only become larger and more frayed during washing.

A LITTLE TALK ABOUT DETERGENTS.

For best results, use liquid detergents in a cold water wash. If you are using powders, pre-dissolve them in a cup of hot water before pouring them into the wash. This distributes the detergent more evenly throughout the the washload.

IF YOUR LEATHER BELT HAS GOTTEN DIRTY, HERE'S A WAY TO CLEAN IT WITHOUT AN EXPENSIVE DRY CLEANING BILL.

Take some cold cream, the kind you use to take off your makeup, and, using a sponge that is well wrung out, rub gently into the leather until it is soft and supple. Then, take a clean cloth and wipe away the cold cream. Presto! Your belt will be clean and supple.

WANT A QUICK WAY TO PERK UP THE VEIL ON YOUR OLD HAT SO THAT IT WILL BE AS GOOD AS NEW? TRY THIS.

First, set your hat on some clean paper. Then take a can of hair spray or artist's fixative and spray a light stream over the veil. You can also use a fresh hand towel to place between the hat and the veil portion, so that you spray only on the veil. The veil should be fresh and stay in place without that "wilted" look.

IF YOU'RE TEMPTED TO USE A FABRIC SOFTENER ON YOUR COTTON TOWELS AND WASHCLOTHS TO GET THEM SUPER SOFT, BE WARNED.

Although using a softener does make your bath linen very soft, it has a drawback, too. At the same time that it is softening, it has a chemical that can make the towels and washcloths less absorbent. So—be sure not to overuse this product.

A WORD OR TWO ABOUT BLEACH.

First of all, be careful! Bleach is extremely strong and can even act as a solvent, destroying your clothes if too much is used or it is left in contact with the garments for too long a time.

Remember to bleach your clothes only in the wash cycle, so that they can be rinsed out thoroughly during the rinse cycle.

AND, ANOTHER WORD ABOUT BLEACH...

Never, ever pour bleach directly into your machine onto your wash load! Direct contact like that may leave spot or bleach "stains". Instead, add the liquid to the wash water first before putting in the clothes.

FABRIC SOFTENERS CAN BE JUST AS "DANGEROUS" AS BLEACH.

Always read the fabric softener instructions, as different brands get added at different times in the wash cycle.

TOO MUCH FABRIC SOFTENER CAN "SPOIL" YOUR WASH.

By "spoil", I mean simply, that on towels and diapers, and numerous other things that you wash, too much fabric softener can cause build-up, make the article feel slick, and fight absorbancy. Because of these things, try using your softener on every third load.

WHEN YOU BLEACH WHITE LINEN OR COTTON, BE CAREFUL TO FOLLOW THE DIRECTIONS VERY CAREFULLY. DON'T MAKE THE MISTAKE OF THINKING THAT MORE IS BETTER.

Although it may be very tempting to add more than the suggested amount of bleach when you are washing your linen or cotton garments, in order to get them cleaner than clean, don't add more than the amount that is suggested on your bleach product. Overuse of bleach is likely to weaken the fibers and this can result in a shorter life span for your clothing.

EVEN WHEN THE LABEL SAYS THAT IT'S OK TO WASH, TEST YOUR SILK CLOTHING FIRST BEFORE GOING AHEAD.

Even if the manufacturer states that it is fine to wash your silk garment, don't be sorry! Before washing the entire garment, take a small piece, one that is well out of sight when the garment is being worn, and test it to make sure that it does not bleed. Then, and only then, should you proceed to do the entire garment.

EVEN WHEN YOUR SILK BLOUSE PROVES ITSELF WASHABLE, DON'T WASH IT TOO VIGOROUSLY.
Remember, even though it may be washable, silk is still considered a very delicate fabric. So, be very careful when you wash—don't scrub vigorously, but gently swish the garment through the washing solution.

WHEN LOADING YOUR WASHER, REMEMBER THIS....
Mix large garments with small items in each wash load, for the best circulation. Remember to distribute them evenly around the agitator or washbasket. Load the washer to capacity, but don't *over* load, or you'll find that your wash won't get as clean as it should.

HERE'S A QUICK TIP TO KEEP SOCKS TOGETHER.
Buy a small open mesh wash bag and put your socks into it when laundering them. You won't lose any this way, and you'll find that this little trick works great for underwear and any small or delicate items.

WHEN WASHING A LINEN GARMENT, BE SURE TO IRON WHEN STILL SLIGHTLY DAMP.
Linen is a particularly difficult fabric to iron, because it is so heavy in weight. Therefore, the best way to iron this fabric is when it is still damp—before it has dried completely. Use an iron that is set for "Linen", which is usually a hot setting. Move the iron slowly back and forth over the garment, making sure that you finish one area before moving on to the next.

IF YOU ARE GOING TO SEW A COTTON DRESS FROM SCRATCH, AVOID SHRINKAGE LATER ON. WASH THE RAW FABRIC FIRST.
Cotton is particularly notorious for shrinkage, and thus, when you are planning to sew a dress from scratch, it is advisable to wash the fabric first, thus pre-shrinking it and ensuring that the dimensions that you sew are the dimensions that will remain in your garment for its lifetime.

IF YOU ARE CLEANING FELT FABRIC, BE SURE NOT TO WET THE FELT TOO MUCH.

Felt is a fabric that is very subject to shrinkage. If you need to clean any garment or other felt item, use only a damp sponge. Felt can be cleaned very well, but it does require care to make sure that it holds its size and shape.

EVEN THOUGH IT MAY BE TEMPTING TO TRY TO BLEACH YOUR WOOL SWEATERS, DON'T MAKE THAT MISTAKE. YOU WILL END UP WITH ONE LESS SWEATER THAN YOU PREVIOUSLY OWNED.

Wool is a fabric that *cannot* be bleached, so no matter how tempting it is to pour on the bleach, don't do it.

THE IN'S AND OUT'S OF DRYING YOUR CLOTHES.

Always shake out your clothes when you take them out of the washer. It eliminates excessive moisture and cuts drying time by at least a third. Also, it'll cut down on wrinkles, which may mean that many things won't need ironing, and isn't that the best news of all?

DON'T STUFF YOUR DRYER FULL OF WET CLOTHING!

Of course they'll get dry, but they'll also be badly wrinkled and they don't dry evenly, *and* they'll take about twice as long to dry, which won't do your budget any good! So, although it may *seem* to take longer, the reality is that you'll cut ironing time, and save on your utility bill, too!

WHEN HANGING YOUR HAND WASH TO DRY, DO THIS.

Before hanging your hand wash up to dry, try this. Lay the freshly hand-laundered garment on a towel, flat out. Roll the item in the towel and gently squeeze to remove excess moisture. It'll cut down the drying time tremendously.

SOME THINGS SHOULDN'T BY DRIED IN THE DRYER.

Never dry anything plastic or foam rubber in the dryer. Never machine dry anything wool, either. Also, try not to use high temperatures when drying synthetics. Although most are machine dryable, at high temperatures they can almost literally "melt"!

EVEN IF YOUR WOOL SWEATER IS ABLE TO BE WASHED IN THE MACHINE, DON'T AUTOMATICALLY ASSUME THAT YOU CAN PUT IT IN THE DRYER.

Wool garments are sometimes fine for machine washing, but a large percentage of these cannot be dried in a commercial dryer. Be sure to check the label very carefully, because if you mistakenly dry a garment that is not suggested for a dryer, you can end up with a ruined sweater!

IF YOU NEED TO PRESS YOUR WOOL GARMENT, BE SURE TO USE A PRESS CLOTH.

Whenever you must iron wool, be sure to set your iron on its steam setting, and then use a press cloth. The least costly press cloth can be made of an old white sheet or pillowcase. This should be soaked in warm water, and then wrung as dry as possible. The press cloth should be set on the garment in small patches, and then the iron touches only the press cloth, sending the steam indirectly to the wool. Once the entire garment is pressed, hang in the open air to allow the steam to thoroughly dry out. Then you'll be ready to store in the closet.

BE CAREFUL NOT TO PUT YOUR WOOLEN SWEATERS AWAY UNLESS THEY ARE CLEAN AND TREATED FOR MOTHS.

It is a very sorry matter when you go to retrieve your sweaters after a long summer to find that they have small moth holes in them. Don't be sure that moths won't attack your favorites. The only way to prevent this for certain is to clean your sweaters and then mothproof them. Store them with a sufficient supply of mothballs and you'll never have regrets. Too many times carelessness results in ruined wool garments. A little caution goes a long way.

WASHING YOUR DOWN COAT AT HOME?

Good idea, and a money-saving one, too, judging by the price of dry-cleaning lately. There are, however, some things to remember when caring for your down clothing at home. Always remember, that excessive wringing, while it may get the water out, will also break-down the down or fiber-fill, and cause your garment to be less warm and may seriously reduce the "life" expectancy of your coat.

MORE ABOUT WASHING DOWN COATS...

Before washing a down coat, always be sure to zip all zippers and close all closures, to prevent any rips, snags or punctures.

AND EVEN MORE ABOUT DOWN...

Before washing any down or fiber-fill garment or throw, remember to look for and repair all rips, tears or holes, or you'll be facing a washer full of feathers at the end of the cycle.

AND FINALLY, ABOUT DRYING THOSE WARMING DOWN GARMENTS...

When drying your down garment, *never* dry them on a hot temperature. Instead, let them dry slowly, in a cool or moderate dryer. It will increase the longevity of the garment and also protect its' beauty. Also, throw in a clean tennis to keep the coat moving inside the dryer and to fluff up the coat!

WHEN YOU SOAK ACETATE FABRIC, BE SURE TO SEPARATE WHITE GARMENTS FROM COLORED ONES.

Acetate is particularly apt to run, so be sure to separate the white from the colored garments.

WHEN WEARING ACETATE FABRICS, BE SURE NOT TO SPRAY YOUR PERFUME ON THE GARMENT DIRECTLY.

Although it may seem very appealing, when you are wearing acetate, do not spray your favorite perfume directly onto the fabric. Acetate is very easily ruined by the chemicals in perfumes, so be sure to spray directly on your skin, preferably before putting on the garment. Then allow the perfume to dry thoroughly before getting your acetate garment into place.

ALTHOUGH ACETATE LOOKS LIKE IT MIGHT TAKE A VERY HOT IRON, IT DOESN'T!

When ironing your acetate garments, you should set the iron on the very lowest possible setting. It is best to iron acetate before it dries completely, and, to ensure that you don't scorch it, even with the low setting, iron on the reverse side. That way, you'll ensure the fabric every chance of survival.

WHAT IF THE ACETATE JUST DOESN'T IRON WELL ON THE WRONG SIDE?

Then you may iron on the right side, but be sure to use a press cloth. That will protect the acetate.

DIAPERS MAY BE THE HARDEST THING TO KEEP LOOKING CLEAN, FRESH, AND NEW.

If you have a child still in diapers, you know what a chore it is to keep those diapers looking like anything *but* nasty, stained and ugly. Well, the first thing to remember is never to use ammonia on soiled diapers. Instead, try this: sponge a little mixture of white-wine vinegar and bleach onto the offensive area. Let it soak, and then launder as usual.

ALWAYS USE YOUR MEASURING CUP.

When doing the laundry, always use your measuring cup. Economic reasons aside, it is best to measure, because too little detergent will not get your clothes clean. Too much will not rinse out properly and will help in the break-down of fibers.

IF YOU WANT TO GET YOUR WASH REALLY CLEAN...

Remember to turn your pockets inside out, to make sure all "debris" washes out. This is particularly important if you have kids!

SHOE POLISH STAINS CAN BE LIFTED.

That is, if you act in time. A shoe polish stain can really mar the looks of a white garment, but here's a quick method for removing those pesty spots. Simply pour on, straight from the bottle, rubbing alcohol! If the clothing is colored, dilute it first, using a solution of two parts distilled water to one part rubbing alcohol. and you'll be spotless in no time.

HERE'S A SCORCHING TALE OF WOE.
How many times have you been in a mad rush and accidently scorched your favorite white blouse or maybe even his best white dress shirt? Well, if you thought those "stains" were permanent, think again. If the garment is all cotton, simply soak a clean cotton rag in peroxide, the three-percent solution that all drug stores sell. Gently sponge the stain away and then launder as usual. Presto, no more embarassing scorch marks.

FRESHEN YOUR LAUNDRY!
Make everyone think you've washed and dried your clothes in the open air and sunshine, and also get them cleaner than they've been in a long time. How? Easy; just add a half cup of regular ammonia to the next wash load. It'll get your clothes really clean and smelling their freshest ever.

BE CAREFUL ABOUT USING CHLORINE BLEACHES ON YOUR NYLON FABRICS.
You must be very careful to test the nylon garment you plan to wash before you actually wash it. And, if it is not colorfast, do NOT use any chlorine bleach on it. This is very important, because the misuse of chlorine can seriously damage your fine nylon garments.

KEEP YOUR WHITE NYLON GARMENTS SEPARATE!
Never, never mix white nylon garments with colored fabric of any kind. This is very important, because you can easily ruin the bright white nylon color of your clothing if you fail to observe this rule.

GOOD NEWS ...
IF YOUR NYLON GARMENTS ARE OF THE DURABLE TYPE, THEY DON'T NEED TO BE HAND-WASHED.
For the nylon garments which you have which are more durable, you can feel safe in using a general laundry detergent and machine washing in warm water. Just be careful to follow the

directions on the box of the laundry detergent, to be sure that you use the correct cycle and amount of soap.

IF YOUR NYLON FABRICS GATHER A LOT OF ELECTRICITY, TRY THIS TRICK.

Nylon fabrics are notorious for producing a lot of static electricity. The best way to combat this is with the use of a good fabric softener. Check the directions on the softener to be sure that it is recommended for use with nylon.

DOUBLE-KNIT FABRICS REALLY HOLD IN DIRT AND GREASY STAINS, BUT HERE'S A QUICK TIP TO GET THEM OUT.

If you've gotten a greasy stain on one of your double-knits, never fear. No matter if you're at home or in a restaurant, just sponge the stained area clean with good old club soda!

HAND-WASHING GOT YOU DOWN?

Well, cheer up! It probably isn't the hand-washing that's got you down, but the endless rinsing. Just add a 1/4 cup of white-wine vinegar to the rinse water and it'll cut your rinsing time in half.

SPEAKING OF HAND-WASHING...

If your hand-washables "bleed" or have a tendency to fade, just add a little old-fashioned Epsom salts to the rinse water, and most types of fabrics will hold their color.

HAND-WASHING SWEATERS IS A LOT CHEAPER THAN DRY CLEANING.

However, so often the sweaters start to feel itchy or look, well, just not new any more. Here's a quick tip that'll keep your sweaters looking and feeling their best. From your drug-store, get a small bottle of glycerine. Add a drop or two to the rinse water and your woolens will be like new.

IF EVERYONE IN YOUR FAMILY IS AS MESSY AS MINE, HERE'S A GREAT TIP THAT'LL SAVE YOU A FORTUNE IN DRY CLEANING BILLS.

Did you know that most spot removers currently being marketed could be made safely at home in your own laundry? It's easy! Just mix one part superior rubbing alcohol with two parts H_2O, and presto!, instant spot remover.

INK STAINS ARE JUST ABOUT THE HARDEST SPOTS TO REMOVE.
However, here's a fast way to clean that nasty spot out. Simply spray on a little hairspray, and brush lightly with a new, firm tooth brush before washing the garment in your usual way.

GREASE STAINS DON'T NECESSARILY MEAN THAT YOU HAVE TO THROW YOUR GARMENT AWAY.
Instead, try this before you launder your grease-stained clothing. Apply a little warm club soda, first. Soak the stain in the soda and then wash as usual.

HOW LONG DO YOUR KID'S WHITE SOCKS STAY WHITE?
Well, if they are like most kids, not too long. However, to whiten those grungy socks, add half a cup of lemon juice to the wash, and they'll sparkle like new. Try it on his white dress shirts for similar results.

PILLOWS GET DIRTY, TOO!
Many people never wash their feather pillows, but it can be done, and easily, too! First, check that all the seams are secure and there are no holes, or you'll be up to your ears in feathers in no time! Next, wash only one pillow at a time, adding towels to balance the load. Be sure to let the washer fill with warm water first before putting the pillow in, and be certain to wash only on "gentle". Stop the washer about half way through its' cycle and flip the pillow over, so that both sides get cleaned. Always dry pillows on the lowest temperature setting possible and be forwarned that the drying time could be as high as two or three hours. However, there is nothing like sleeping on fresh, clean pillows.

HAS YOUR WASHER EVER "SUDSED-OVER"?
Well, if it has, then you know what a mess that can be. The next time, try adding a tablespoon or two of fabric softener & suds will disappear!

ONE OF THE WORST STAINS TO GET OUT IS BLOOD.

The important thing to remember with a blood stain, however, is to act fast. If possible, soak the stained garment in cold water immediately. Let it soak for a half an hour or more. Next gently rub the stain against another part of the fabric, working it in your hands, along with a little hydrogen peroxide (be sure the garment is color fast) and a drop or two of ammonia. Rinse the stained area thoroughly and then launder the garment as you always would.

CHEWING GUM CAN BE A REAL CLOTHES RUINER ...

but, it doesn't have to be. The next time your little one gets gum all over his or her best clothes, try this. Just put the garment into a plastic freezer bag and throw it in the freezer for an hour. When the gum is hardened, carefully pick it off. A gentle brush-up with any cleaning fluid afterward, will get the last die-hard pieces off.

RUST MAY NEVER SLEEP, BUT HERE'S A WAY TO PUT IT IN DREAMLAND.

Rust stains are really difficult. Because of this, many people try to get them out with bleach. This is a serious error. *Bleach will set the stain permanently*! Instead, try a little cool, distilled water and lemon juice, and then allow the garment to dry naturally in the sun.

COFFEE OR TEA STAINS?

Don't let them get you down. Sponge the area off with cool water. Use your fingers to work an ordinary dishwashing detergent into the area. Sponge the stain clean, and then rinse under cool, running water.

DON'T THROW THAT TABLE-CLOTH AWAY, GET THOSE WINE STAINS OUT!

Red wine can really ruin a table cloth, but the next time someone spills on your favorite, remember this: salt! Yes, common table salt, will "absorb" the stain. Then, simply rinse under cold running water and wash the cloth as you normally would.

TAR CAN BE A REALLY STICKY PROBLEM.

However, try sponging it off with dry cleaning fluid, straight from the can, before it has a chance to dry.

STUBBORN FOOD STAINS?

Well, just pre-soak the stained clothes in a heavy solution of warm water and automatic-dishwashing soap, before laundering them as usual.

DO YOUR CLOTHES RUN?

Well, you can make them colorfast via this simple and quick solution, no pun intended. Just soak them for a few minutes in a solution of warm water, white vinegar, and sea salt.

WASHED YOUR BEST WOOL SWEATER BY MISTAKE?

To be truthful, there isn't that much that can be done. However, if the sweater isn't too badly shrunken, you might try this: plop that shriveled-up mass of once proud wool into a strong solution of cool water and your favorite shampoo. Rinse thoroughly, and try to re-block the garment on a smooth surface it can dry on. Good luck!

RING AROUND THE COLLAR, RING AROUND THE COLLAR!

You've tried... well, if you're like us, probably everything! Here's one that works, though. A little ordinary hair shampoo on that oily dirt will do the trick.

YOUR WASHER GETS DIRTY, TOO!

Most of us seem to forget that the washer gets dirty, too. And, a clean machine is a happy machine. So, to clean your washing machine, simply run it through the regular cycle, but add a half gallon of white, distilled vinegar.

VINEGAR IS GOOD FOR MANY THINGS IN THE LAUNDRY ROOM.

For instance, it makes a fine, clean-smelling rinse for your clothes, and white vinegar takes the suds out, too!

LINT GOT YOU DOWN?

Nothing is more depressing than removing your freshly laundered clothes from the washer and finding them covered with lint. Next time, while the clothes are still damp (not wet), simply brush them with a regular clothes brush. If the thought of all that work is even more depressing to you, here's a quicker and much, much easier solution. Take an old nylon netting potato bag, (you know, the kind you get potatoes in at the grocery) and after making sure it's clean and all paper and tags have been removed, throw it in the dryer with your wet clothes and it'll act as a clothing brush for you.

MORE TALES OF LINT AND WOE.

However, if you want to eliminate the lint at it's source, just try this: Add a full cup of that most useful of all household items, white-wine vinegar, to the final rinse. Your clothes will emerge from the washer lint free!

BOOZE STAINS WILL TURN BROWN WITH AGE.

So, even though the alcohol spilled was colorless, a nasty brown stain may show up later. Consequently, it is best to treat the stain while it's still fresh. Use cold water and a few drops of glycerine to loosen most alcohol stains. Next, rinse the area clean with a mild solution of cool water and white-wine vinegar. When the area is clean, rinse again with cold water.

LINE-DRYING CLOTHES IS AN "ART FORM" ALL UNTO ITSELF.

By that I mean, that there are many subtleties to learn before drying clothes the old-fashioned way, but that fresh clean smell is worth it. For instance, always remember to dry colored or dark clothing out of direct sunshine, in the shade. Whites *should* be hung in the sun, however.

AND WHAT ABOUT YOUR CLOTHESLINE?

A dirty clothesline will leave your freshly laundered clothes dirty, too. So, simply run a dampened cloth over the line before hanging out the clothes to dry.

HERE'S A HINT TO MAKE YOUR LAUNDRY SPARKLE.
Just add a half cup of powdered borax to regular soap powder
and your clothes will look really clean, and they'll smell fresh
and great, too.

MAKE-UP STAINS CAN BE REMOVED, TOO!

Although no method of make-up stain removal is fool-proof, or
100% successful, this is the best we've found. Spread the area of
the stain with a thin coating of vaseline. Next, use any household
grease-cutter and a Q-tip swab to gently work the stain out.

FLOORS
and
FURNITURE

INTRODUCTION FOR FLOORS AND FURNITURE

Ever feel overwhelmed by the prospect of cleaning and maintaining those beautiful wood floors and that expensive piece of furniture? This chapter is for you because it provides easy and inexpensive ways to maintain floors and furniture, and we tell you what kinds of cleaning agents are safe to use and what kinds to avoid in order to preserve your fine floors and furniture in the best possible condition.

We give you tips on how to clean carpets yourself. We even provide instructions for removing scratches from wood, plus, all sorts of extras for those sudden disasters—how to remove gum from your beloved carpeting, how to make water marks disappear from furniture, and how to get crayon coloring off no-wax floors. In short, there are easy-to-follow instructions for all your floor and furniture care needs—instructions that will save you time and energy, and keep your home looking great.

WANT TO AVOID THAT LITTLE HOUSE ON THE PRAIRIE LOOK WITH YOUR WOOD FLOORS?

Remember, wood floors will clean up nicely if you just run a dust mop over them every few days. Water should never be used directly on wood floors because they can warp and rot. If you do need to do more than dust, take a damp cloth (thoroughly wrung out) and go over the floor and then dry with another cloth.

WHAT KIND OF CLEANERS CAN I USE ON MY NEW LINOLEUM FLOOR?

First, be sure that it is *linoleum*. Many new floors are really vinyl, and the only commercial products safe to use are those that specifically state "for no-wax floors". Usually vinyl floors can retain their beauty and shine if you are simply careful to wipe up spills as they occur and damp mop as necessary.

CARPETING CAN BE CLEANED REGULARLY AND INEXPENSIVELY SIMPLY BY USING SOME HANDY HOME METHODS.

To perk up the color of your carpet, simply sprinkle with salt and vacuum. To deodorize, sprinkle with baking soda and vacuum, or vacuum and then spray with a light coating of Lysol (do not walk on the carpet until dry).

ARE SCRATCHES DISFIGURING YOUR PARQUET FLOORS?

To spruce them up, try a coat of floor wax on light scratches. For deeper scratches, rub gently with steel wool, clean and wax. (Sometimes, you may need to touch up the color of the scratched area by using a small artist's paint brush and some wood stain.)

WHEN YOU WASH YOUR LAMPSHADE, USE THIS TRICK TO PREVENT THE FRAME FROM RUSTING.

You must be careful that your lampshade frame doesn't rust after it is wet, so the best method is to hasten the drying process by use of a hand-held hair dryer. You should not hold it too close to the fabric, however, to avoid scorching, and the best way is to use it on the "low" setting.

CHECK YOUR LAMP SHADE BEFORE WASHING TO AVOID DISASTER.

You must be sure, before washing a lampshade, that the shade is not glued to the frame. If glue has been used, water will loosen the frame and you'll have a disaster. So, if your shade has been glued to the frame, you must have the shade dry-cleaned.

WHEN WASHING A LAMPSHADE, CHECK THAT TRIM!

Sometimes your lampshade can be sewed to the frame, but it may have trim that has been glued on. If this is the case, never wash the shade, for the trim will separate from the shade.

NATURAL SUN DRYING IS WONDERFUL, BUT NOT FOR YOUR SILK LAMPSHADES.

If you have fine silk lampshades, allow them to dry in the house or the shade, but never in the sun. Fine silk is very fragile, and should never be left drying in the sun.

CAN HEAT MARKS AND BURNS ON FURNITURE BE REPAIRED WITHOUT REFINISHING THE WHOLE THING?

Yes, they can! Use a very sharp knife to scrape away the burned wood. Next, use a match to heat the end of a laquer stick (available in almost any hardware or paint store) and with a broad, smooth knife, work the laquer into the hole. Wait until it hardens, and then sand lightly with a fine grade of sand paper. Use a crayon to color in the area and wax as usual.

HERE'S HOW YOU CAN GET BLACK RUBBER HEEL MARKS OFF YOUR BEAUTIFUL HARDWOOD FLOORS.

Mineral spirits, applied with a damp cloth, will do the trick.

IS THERE ANYTHING THAT CAN BE DONE ABOUT A SQUEAKING BED?

Of course. Just drop a few drops of any liquid soap into the slats and the squeak will disappear.

HOW CAN THE OLD LAQUER BE STRIPPED OFF A BRASS BED AND THE BED CLEANED AND POLISHED?

Just use regular paint thinner, and clean cloths. After you've stripped off all the old laquer, polish the bed with brass polish and it will look clean and new. Warning: if the bed is not coated with laquer again, or a clear plastic sealer, it will tarnish and need more polishing.

CUT DOWN ON YOUR VACUUMING WITH THIS EASY PREVENTIVE MEASURE.

The best way to prevent excessive vacuuming is to keep mats at the front and back entrances to absorb the soil that comes in. A mat will keep most of the dirt from ever reaching your carpet. Then, most of your cleaning effort will actually be for the mat!

WHEN YOUR CARPET NEEDS EXPERT CLEANING, STEAM EXTRACTION REALLY WORKS.

Steam extraction machines are really the best for carpets which have become heavily dirty. This, combined with a rotary method, will bring your carpet back to a fresh condition.

WHEN YOUR CARPET IS NEW OR FRESHLY CLEANED, HERE'S A WAY TO HELP KEEP IT THAT WAY.

There are products on the market which actually help to prevent soil from settling into your carpet. They help to slow the accumulation of dirt and stains and will keep your carpet cleaner between professional cleaning jobs. With this protector, you will need only to vacuum and clean up any spots which occur.

TEST CARPET SHAMPOO BEFORE YOU USE IT.

Before you actually apply a carpet shampoo to your carpeting, test it. Put some in a saucer or bowl and allow it to dry. If there is a sticky film, this will be the film on your carpet, and will attract soil. A good shampoo will have a powdery rather than a sticky residue.

DON'T THROW OLD TEA BAGS AWAY, USE THEM TO PUT A SHINE OF YOUR FLOORS.

Save your old tea bags. Make tea with them again and rub the tea into your varnished floors and woodwork. It'll give the wood a great shine.

WHAT ABOUT SPOTTED AND FADED HARDWOOD FLOORS?

Here's a neat trick. Just mix a little ordinary brown shoe polish into your liquid floor wax and polish the floors evenly. They'll look old-fashioned, lovely and even!

WHAT ABOUT SQUEAKY FLOORS?

Simple! Just empty a little baby powder into the cracks, let it settle and the squeak will be gone.

WHAT ABOUT SMALL BLACK HEEL MARKS?

For "touch-ups", try using an art gum eraser.

HOW CAN I GET THE KID'S CRAYON MARKS OFF MY NO-WAX FLOORS? HELP!!!

As strange as it may sound, try using a little silver polish. It works every time.

HERE'S A QUICK METHOD FOR DUSTING INTRICATE VICTORIAN OR OTHER ANTIQUE FURNITURE.

If you've ever dusted carved and intricate antique furniture, you know how time consuming it can be. Well, fret no more. Buy a new, soft-bristle paint brush, spray it with a dust-attracting spray, and dusting will take half the time it used to.

MAKE YOUR GLASS TOP COFFEE TABLES SPARKLE.

Cleaning glass top tables is usually no fun, mostly because the lint from your cloth creates as much work as it takes care of. Well, here's the solution. Just mix a little home-made solution of warm water and your favorite laundry fabric softener. You'll find your tables lint-free and sparkling.

CHROME TABLES NEED A QUICK PICK-ME-UP?

Club soda is a cheap and easy way to put a shine back onto your chrome.

HERE'S A QUICK PICK-UP TREATMENT FOR PESTY DUSTBALLS.

Actually, it's simple. A damp mop will pick up twice as much dust as a dry one. And twice as quickly.

FOR YOUR FINE WOOD ANTIQUES, NOTHING SHINES BETTER THAN A GOOD PASTE WAX.

In order to maintain the fine flow of your antique wood, nothing can do it better than a good paste wax. All you need to do is apply the paste wax and let it dry. Then buff to a fine burnished shine.

WHEN YOU SPRAY YOUR WOOD FURNITURE, MAKE SURE THAT YOU DO *ONLY* THE FURNITURE. DON'T MAKE EXTRA JOBS FOR YOURSELF.

It can happen that when you use a spray wax on your furniture, that you allow some of the spray to get on the upholstered portions, or even the painted walls. Be careful not to let this happen, because you'll then have to clean the walls or other affected areas. Keep your work as simple as possible.

USE CARE WITH YOUR PLASTIC FURNITURE— AVOID THAT CLOUDY LOOK.

Plastic furniture should never be cleaned with ammonia or any product that has an alcohol base. This will result in a surface that is very cloudy. So, regular dusting or cleaning with a general cleaning agent is the best.

DON'T USE YOUR FAVORITE DETERGENT ON YOUR LEATHER UPHOLSTERY.

Leather should never be cleaned with detergent. Use only a mild soap product in order to keep your leather supple and prevent it from drying out.

IN ORDER TO KEEP YOUR FLOORS LOOKING THEIR BEST, DAMP-MOP THEM EVERY DAY.

In order to keep your floors looking clean and shiny, simply use a dampened mop every day. Use some mild cleanser in warm water and your floors will stay in prime condition longer.

CONCRETE FLOORS COLLECT A LOT OF DIRT, AND THE ONLY SOLUTION IS TO SEAL YOUR CONCRETE FLOOR.

No matter how many times you mop or sweep your concrete floor, it will be constantly accumulating dust. Even when you vacuum it, after any use, it will just be as dusty as ever. So the only solution is to seal your concrete floors. Take up all the surface dirt and make sure the floor is clear of all furniture. Use an alkaline cleaner in a strong solution. Allow this to remain on the floor for several hours so that it will clean the lime on the top of the concrete. Then rinse well. After allowing your floor to dry for approximately 12 hours, apply a concrete sealer in an even coat, and allow it to dry thoroughly. Then, when the first coat is completely dry, use a second coat. You will have a floor which can be cleaned as if it were a regular hard floor, and you will save countless hours of useless sweeping and vacuuming.

INSTEAD OF SANDING YOUR OLD WOOD FLOORS, TRY THIS METHOD.

When you sand your old wood floors, you just create a mess. So, instead, use varnish remover on your floor. This will cause the old finish to break up and you can use a squeegee to get rid of the cracked varnish.

BUFF THAT DINING ROOM TABLE

If you've got a lovely old dining room table made of good wood, invest in a quality buffer that you would use for shoes. Then buff your table to a high luster.

IF YOU HAVE FLOOR REGISTERS

If you're distressed about the amount of dust that comes out of your floor register, try any of the following. Cut up an old piece of mesh screening, or stretch an old nylon stocking over the register.

REMOVING WATERSPOTS FROM WOOD FURNITURE

As distressing as it seems to have an ugly water ring or spot on good wood furniture, something can be done about it without refinishing the wood. Use plain cornstarch. Apply an ample portion over the area to be worked on. Leave it sit for several hours. Wipe up and repeat the process if necessary.

CORNSTARCH IS GOOD FOR YOUR FURNITURE

Besides treating water marks, a light sprinkling of cornstarch on waxed furniture is a great way to pick up excess oils. Buff with a soft cloth and watch that wood shine.

CARING FOR YOUR DINING ROOM TABLE (AND OTHER GOOD TABLES)

If you have good furniture, such as wood, marble, lacquer, etc., and if it's kept in sunny rooms, you should turn the table every few months. That way the material will fade evenly.

HELP! IS THERE ANY WAY TO GET NAIL POLISH OFF OF TILE OR LINOLEUM FLOORS?

First of all, unlike most spills, let the nail polish dry before attempting to remove it. Once it's tacky, you can peel up most of it. The leftover polish can be removed with (surprise!) a watered down solution of nail polish remover.

HERE'S HOW TO GIVE YOUR FLOORS A QUICK SHINE.
Just wrap your broom or mop with wax paper and give your floors the once over.

IS THERE ANY WAY TO GET RID OF THOSE MARKS THE ROCKER LEAVES ON THE WOODEN FLOORS?
One way, that's good, fast, and simple, is to polish the "arcs" of the rocker when you polish the floors!

CHROME FURNITURE CAN LOOK GOOD AS NEW
When you're finished with the aluminum foil pieces in your kitchen, save the clean ones. Then, the next time you're polishing furniture, use leftover pieces of foil, that have been dampened slightly to rub down the chrome. The shiny side should face out and the foil should turn black while the chrome turns shiny.

TABLE EXTENSIONS
If you've got table extenders that you hardly ever use (except for those rare occasions when the whole family gets together), don't leave them in a dark closet. Either take them out and insert them into the table and leave them there for a few weeks, or leave them out in the same room so they get a chance to fade to the same color as the rest of the table.

LOOSE FLOOR TILES CAN BE TIGHTENED
Take a cotton dishtowel and place it over the loose tile. Iron it with an iron set on the heaviest setting. If it's in real bad condition, you should be able to lift up the tile and add some extra glue. If not, start immediately with the next step. Lay some heavy books down right after the ironing process. The heat should loosen the glue and the weight of the books should help to "reset" it.

THE PRICE OF A COMMERCIAL BUCKET FOR YOUR MOP IS GOOD INSURANCE AGAINST CUTS ON YOUR HANDS.

You can prevent cuts on your hands that come from small bits of broken bottles or other foreign objects that your mop gathers by purchasing a bucket that has a built-in wringer. Thus, instead of using your hands, the metal edges of the wringer do the work for you. These buckets are available in better quality hardware stores, but if your local hardware store does not stock them, try a commercial cleaning supply company.

EVEN WHEN YOUR FLOOR *LOOKS* CLEAN, DON'T BELIEVE THAT IT IS! SWEEP FLOORS WELL TO KEEP THEM IN GOOD CONDITION.

In order to ensure that your floors remain in good condition for many years, coat them with one or two applications of wax. It is usually better to apply several thin coats, rather than one heavy coat, to avoid a heavy coagulation of wax.

BEFORE YOU PUT ON A NEW APPLICATION OF WAX, BE SURE TO REMOVE THE OLD FINISH FIRST.

After your floor is surface clean, mop your floor with a solution of plain water and some ammonia. You can vary the strength of this solution, depending on whether you want to take off just the top coating of wax, or get down to all of the wax. If the wax has built up very heavily, you may need to reapply your ammonia solution.

YOU CAN MAKE DUSTING SOLUTION, AND SAVE MONEY, TOO!

Instead of buying a ready-made dust-attracting spray, why not make your own. Just use your favorite cleaning product to make up a bucket of hot, sudsy water. Next, drop in a couple of teaspoons of regular turpentine. Throw in some clean, cotton dustcloths, stir so that they get saturated, and let them soak for eight or ten hours. After they've soaked, wring them out and hang them up to dry. As soon as they are dry, they're ready to use.

HOW TO TAKE CARE OF YOUR WICKER.

Wicker should be washed in a mild solution of warm (never hot) salt water. This will keep it from yellowing with age.

...AND ANOTHER THING TO REMEMBER WHEN CLEANING YOUR WICKER FURNITURE.

Always wash it indoors, away from the sunlight. When you wash it, soak it down good. To dry, put it out in the sunshine and let the heat and light tighten any sagging parts.

YOUR GARDEN FURNITURE MAY MILDEW WHEN STORED, SO REMEMBER THIS.

Use a mild ammonia and water solution and don't allow the wicker or wood to become saturated; just dampen your cloth and rub it off. That way, your furniture will be mildew free, and you won't have to worry about bleaching out or discoloring the wicker.

NO MATTER HOW MUCH YOU MAY WANT TO BELIEVE IT EXISTS, THE TRUTH IS THAT THERE IS NO SUCH THING AS A NO-WAX FLOOR.

No matter how wonderful the original finish is, as time goes by, every floor will become dull and lose its finish. Particularly if you have children, the foot traffic takes its toll on your floor. All sorts of material can become damaging to the surface of the floor. So be prepared to wax your floors, even if they are supposed to be "no-wax."

EVEN THOUGH "NO-WAX" FLOORS DO NEED WAX, CONSIDER THEM SERIOUSLY WHEN BUYING A FLOOR.

Research has found that no-wax floors do last better than an ordinary vinyl floor. They do need a protective coating, but the upkeep is much easier than the regular variety of floors.

DON'T WAX A FLOOR EVENLY. WAX ACCORDING TO THE TRAFFIC PATTERNS.

When you wax your floor, don't put a heavy coat all over. The areas which receive the most wear and traffic should also get the most wax. Avoid heavy waxing in the corners or the rims of your floors. Also, areas which receive little wear, such as under large pieces of furniture, should only be waxed lightly. That way, you'll avoid the build-up of wax that is never worn and just requires stripping later on.

BE SURE TO USE A COATING OF WAX ON YOUR FLOORS TO GIVE THEM THE MAXIMUM PROTECTION AND ENSURE A LONG LIFE.

Even if your floor is supposedly a "no-wax" floor, it is a good idea to put a coating of wax on the floor. This will prevent excessive wear and tear that comes with heavy traffic or accidental spills. A waxed finish will keep your floor shiny and good-looking, but, in addition, will prevent the damage that may shorten the life of your floor.

IF YOU FIND YOUR FLOOR GETS HEAVY TRAFFIC AND LOTS OF SPILLS, KEEPING IT WAXED WILL MAKE YOUR WORK SHORTER AND EASIER.

Especially if your floor gets a lot of heavy wear, it will be much easier to clean when it has a coat of wax. When your floor is unpolished, the surface will "fight" your broom, and you'll have to work much harder to get your floor clean. Also, you can wipe a spill from small children in no time, because the material stays on top of the wax, and doesn't seep into the flooring.

AS A SAFETY MEASURE, WAX YOUR FLOORS WELL.

It may seem that a shiny floor can contribute to slips and spills, but actually, the exact opposite is true. Unwaxed floors are very hard and don't provide any "give". With a thin, clear coat of wax, your floors will become more slip-resistant and offer you protection.

TOO MUCH WAX? IT CAN BE WORSE THAN NO WAX AT ALL.

However, you can remove waxy build-up in a variety of simple ways. First, you can use a wax that is formulated to strip old wax away. However, if the build-up is substantial, you should use mineral spirits. Use a soft, clean cotton cloth. Soak the cloth with mineral spirits and "attack" one area at a time. When the wax is softened, take another cloth and wipe it away. You can then move on to another part of the piece of furniture.

BUT, WHAT ABOUT SMALL NICKS AND SCRATCHES?
The easiest bet to cover small nicks and scratches is to buy a brown crayon and "color" the scratch in, in the appropriate shade. You can then polish over the coloring and your furniture will look good as new.

WATER MARKS CAN MAKE A LASTING IMPRESSION ON YOUR FURNITURE.
But, they don't have to. The easiest method of removal is as follows: cover the water mark with a thick layer of cigarette or cigar ash. Next, with a clean cloth that has been saturated with cooking oil, (your favorite brand) work the ash into the water mark in a circular motion.

DON'T WAX FLOORS IN THE RAIN
When the humidity is high, it takes extra long for the floors to dry. While they are in that "gummy" state, they are a lot more likely to pick up excess dirt.

SHINE UP YOUR DUSTPAN
Spray on some furniture polish on occasion. You'll see how much more easily the dirt slides off when you go to empty it.

IF YOU'VE GOT A SOFT BROOM
Give it extra life by soaking the bristles in warm water for twenty minutes. Let dry and you'll have stiffer bristles.

CARPET SWEEPERS ARE GREAT FOR SURFACE CLEANING, BUT DON'T MAKE THE MISTAKE OF THINKING THAT THEY REALLY DO THE JOB.
If you love your carpet sweeper because it gets rid of dirt from your carpet or floor so quickly and easily, be aware that this is just an illusion. It is true that you can get a clean look quickly, but they don't reach down into the rug pile the way a good vacuum does. So save them for emergencies only.

YOUR CARPET'S BEST FRIEND IS A BEATER VACUUM.

If you have a carpet, particularly one with a deep pile, the most effective tool is a vacuum with a beater. This is the only tool that can get to the dirt below the surface and get your carpets really clean.

IF YOUR FLOOR IS FULL OF PITTED MARKS, DON'T THINK YOU CAN SCRUB IT CLEAN. BUT YOU CAN DISSOLVE THE MARKS TO REMEDY THE PROBLEM.

The only way to repair a floor that has been a victim of old wax building up is to use a stripping agent that will soften the wax and actually dissolve the dirt right out. You can scrub as much as you want, but all it will do is leave scratch marks.

WHEN SOMEONE DROPS GUM ON YOUR CARPET, YOU NEED CHEMICAL HELP TO REMOVE IT.

Go to your local hardware store and obtain some freon freeze. This will make the gum harden so it can be broken into small removable pieces. Then get rid of the pieces quickly before they get soft again.

A GOOD DUST CLOTH IS HARD TO FIND, OR NEVER THROW A SINGLE SOCK AWAY.

I'm sure you all have experienced the frustration of finding a matchless sock in the clean laundry. Well now you can put that matchless sock to good use. A single cotton sock makes a great dusting mitt! And, they can be used over and over again. You'll wonder how you got along without this wonderful little "tool".

KITCHEN APPLIANCES, COUNTERTOPS and COOKWARE

INTRODUCTION FOR THE KITCHEN

Everyone loves the results of cooking in the kitchen, those tasty aromas of savory main dishes, steaming vegetables, and tempting desserts—but no one is fond of the aftermath—cleaning up after the chef's triumph—and keeping the kitchen area in shining, tip-top shape.

Among these tips and helpful hints for the kitchen, you will find money-saving advice on everything from making your own dish detergent and scouring pads to repairing ceramic counter tops and stopped up sinks. You will find time-savers that help avoid spending hours on burnt pots and pans, and you will find helpful instructions for those dreaded kitchen emergencies.

This chapter will equip you to handle all kitchen problems and minimize the time and effort needed to keep a safe, efficient, and beautiful kitchen. And you'll feel good about your accomplishments and your ability to handle anything in the kitchen from cleaning to repairing.

AN EASY WAY TO GET RID OF YELLOWING ON WHITE KITCHEN APPLIANCES:

Mix up a solution of 1/2 cup household bleach, 1/4 cup baking soda, and 4 cups of water (warm temperature), and wash the appliances. Let them stand in the solution for 10 or 12 minutes before rinsing and drying. Follow the wash with a polish of rubbing alcohol.----Or, if you really want to save time, club soda will both clean and polish white kitchen appliances.

WHAT'S A GOOD WAY TO CLEAN CUTTING AND BREAD BOARDS WITHOUT WARPING THEM?

Use a piece of lemon or fresh lime and rub the fruit across the board. It will get rid of lingering odors from onions or fish, etc.

HERE'S A GREAT WAY TO AVOID SCOURING THE BROILER PAN.

While the pan is still hot cover with a thin layer of laundry detergent and dampened paper towels. Allow to set for a short period of time and then wash the pan. Little to no scouring should be required.

THE BEST WAY TO CLEAN AN ELECTRIC CAN OPENER is to run a paper towel through the cutting process.

HOW TO REMOVE ACCUMULATED BLACK FROM CAST IRON SKILLETS:
Use a store-bought oven cleaner on the bottom and outside of the skillet and allow to stand for around two hours. Then clean with a solution of vinegar and water. Afterward, either warm the skillet and rub the inside with a piece of wax paper a little cooking oil to prevent rusting and hold the seasoning.

COFFEE STAINS CAN RUIN YOUR CERAMIC AND CHINA CUPS
But if you allow them to soak with some warm water and baking soda, you'll reduce that problem. If it's really hard to remove those coffee and tea stains, make a paste out of the baking soda, salt and water. The stains will come right out.

A SWEET SMELLING REFRIGERATOR IS EASY
Use a box of opened baking soda and you'll find that your refrigerator smells sweeter. And here's an extra tip. Although there are lots of decorative ceramics in which to keep the baking soda, it's actually believed that the cardboard box absorbs as much odor as the baking soda.

FINE SCRATCHES IN YOUR WINDOWS, MIRRORS OR OTHER GLASS
Just brush a little bit of toothpaste, rubbing ever so gently, and you'll see an improvement.

IF YOU'VE GOT WOOD FLOORS IN YOUR KITCHEN
There are several ways you should clean them, depending upon whether or not it is unfinished wood. A finished floor should take sudsy water (warm) with a little liquid wax, or if you prefer, paste wax every once in a while. Unfinished floors should be swept. Try not to wash them or wet them except in an emergency.

BRASS AND COPPER THAT REALLY GLEAMS

If you've got a copper and brass collection that you really like to have shining bright, here is a low-cost tip on how to get them to sparkle. Heat up some cider vinegar until hot (1/2 C). Add enough flour to make a paste. Now add salt (3 tbsp) to give the mixture a little abrasiveness. If need be, add some more vinegar. Apply, let dry and buff. You'll be pleased with the results.

ADD SPARKLE TO YOUR GLASSWARE.

The next time you have a sinkful of glasses and china, add 3 tbsp of cider vinegar. Wash in sudsy water as usual. Rinse and sparkle!

CERAMIC TILE COUNTERTOPS NEED EXTRA CARE

Don't put a lot of elbow grease into cleaning them or else you're likely to loosen the tiles. Instead, care for them with a treatment of borax and warm water, made into a liquidy paste. Apply and wipe off with a damp sponge.

IF YOU'VE GOT BAD STAINS ON YOUR CERAMIC TILE..

Try treating them with a paste made of 1 tbsp. of cream of tartar and enough hydrogen peroxide to make a paste. Apply, let dry and wipe off with a clean damp sponge. Don't use a lot of water because it could loosen your tiles.

THROW SALT ON A GREASE FIRE...

If you're mother has ever told you to throw salt on a grease fire, there is a good reason to do so (beyond drowning the flames). Salt will soak up some of the grease and make the mess easier to clean. This is especially helpful when it comes to oven spills which somehow always turn into a real chore to clean up.

DRAINS CLOGGED AND NO COMMERCIAL LIQUID AVAILABLE?

Try this homemade remedy which you are likely to find just as good as the commercial variety. First of all, try to get as much liquid out of the sink or tub. Then pour in this mix: 1/2 C ordinary table salt, 1/2 C baking soda and 1 1/2 tbspon of cream of tartar. Stir and pour gently into the drain followed by 2 C of cold water. Repeat if necessary.

GREASE SPILLS FROM A BAR-BE-CUE
There is nothing more distressing than to see grease spills on a concrete or cement floor because they are so hard to get up. But not if you act immediately. Keep a large box of salt on hand (it's also great to dowse the fire) and immediately pour onto the grease stain. As you see it absorbed, add more. If you haven't got salt, use flour, cornstarch, sawdust, kitty litter. Next day scrub down with sudsy water or baking soda and water.

WANT TO REMOVE TARNISH FROM COPPER POTS AND PANS?
Here are three convenient and easy-to-make methods:
1) Mix a bottle of vinegar with 3 tablespoons of salt and cover pots and pans in the solution, allowing to stand for a half hour or so. The tarnish will simply rub off.
2) Cut a lemon in half and dip one part in salt. Use the salted half to rub the tarnish off.
3) Pour Worcestershire sauce on a soft cloth and rub away the tarnish.

WHAT TO DO ABOUT BURNED AND SCORCHED PANS:
Try one of the following proven methods. First sprinkle the burned portion with a lot of baking soda and add just enough water to dampen it. Let stand for a long time—probably two or three hours at least. Most of the time, the burned part will simply lift out. If however, this does not work, try boiling a mixture of 1 cup water, 2 tablespoons of baking soda, and 1/2 cup vinegar in the burned pot for about 10 or 15 minutes. The burnt on portion should come off.

WHAT'S THE BEST DETERGENT TO USE ON MY DISHES?
The truth is that the best and most efficient detergent to use is the cheapest. Simply add a few drops of vinegar to your dishwater, and your dishes will come as clean as possible.

HOW CAN I GET THOSE COFFEE STAINS OFF MY GOOD CHINA CUPS?

Dip a damp cloth in baking soda and rub the stains away.

WHAT'S A QUICK WAY TO GET BURNED CASSEROLE DISHES CLEAN?

Fill the casserole dish with boiling water and a little baking soda or salt.

KEEP A FRESH-SMELLING KITCHEN

Stick cloves into an orange until it's a solid mass of cloves. Then leave out in the kithen. People are sure to comment on how good it smells.

ANOTHER WAY TO KEEP A FRESH-SMELLING KITCHEN

Boil cinammon bark in water. Keep on a very low simmer. It smells so good, especially in the winter.

KITCHEN SINK STAINS AND YOU'RE IN A HURRY

Moisten paper towels with ordinary household bleach and lay over the stains. Go about your other work for the day. Rinse. Repeat and leave on overnight if necessary.

BUTCHER BLOCK COUNTERS

When they become scratched or discolored, simply give them a light sanding. Then oil with a household cooking oil (other than olive). Wipe all excess oil with a paper towel. Your butcher block will look as good as new.

CHIPPED LAMINATE

Many people don't realize that chipped laminate can be repaired by obtaining a kit (just for this purpose) at the local hardware store.

SHELF LINERS

Many people like to apply decorative self-adhesive coverings to shelves, and then are disappointed that utensils leave unsightly (and often permanent) marks on the paper. Lay down some wax paper as a protector. Throw it away when it's dirty. Or, put a plastic or paper plate under certain items that leave marks.

IRONWARE HAS ITS SPECIAL CARE
Ironware is lovely, but it does tend to show grey scratch marks. Most of the time this is because it is improperly stored. Here are two things you can do. First, get rid of the scratch marks by taking 3 tbsp. of baking soda and adding enough warm water to make a spreadable paste. Rub on and wash off and that should get rid of the marks. Then, store those plates with paper towel or store bought plate dividers so they won't continue to be scratched in the future.

MAKE MIXING GO FASTER
If you're ever annoyed because your ceramic bowls slip on your laminated counter top when you're mixing, put a rubber mat between the bowl and the counter. That will enable you to "anchor" the bowl.

AN ENERGY-SAVING TIP THAT WILL SAVE YOU SCRUBBING POTS AND PANS
Have you ever admired the blue gas flames that lick up the side of a pot as the contents boil away. As nice as it is to have very high heat, it can cause a lot of extra scrubbing. That's because the high heat causes heat stains. For less scrubbing, keep your heat down a little. You'll get the same cooking results, but with less elbow grease.

A TIP FOR REAL BAD POT BURNS
If you're faced with a pot full of black, hardened ash, try this. Boil together 1-1/2 tsp of baking soda and 1-1/4 C of cold water. Boil gently for 20 minutes. Allow to cool. If some scorching still remains, prepare the same solution and let it soak overnight. Then boil gently for another 20 minutes to clean up any residue.

WHEN YOU RUN OUT OF COMMERCIAL SCOURING PADS
Make a paste of baking soda, salt and water. It will do the same

thing as a commercial scouring pad. Use a synthetic scouring pad for a little more abrasion.

IF YOU OWN NEW CLAY COOKERY
Soak it for one hour in hot water (both the bottom and the top) then scrub well with a synthetic scouring pad. This will remove any excess clay dust.

SEASON YOUR IRONWARE
Good (and well cared for) ironware can easily last for many generations. Because cast iron works so well, it's a real pleasure to have. But it does require some maintenance. First of all, clean it gently with sudsy warm water. If it requies any scouring, use a commercial scouring pad (very lightly) and rinse and dry immediately. If any rust spots occur, pour 2 tbsp oil into pan, rub all around with a paper towel, and then put pan on *lowest* heat for 30-45 minutes. This will season the pan and keep it lasting longer.

GIVE YOUR COPPER POT A SWIRL
When heating oil or butter in a copper pot, "swirl" the oil so it coats the bottom *and* some of the side of the pot. This will help prevent scorching.

BE GENTLE WITH COPPER
Remember, copper scratches more easily than many of the materials on the market today. Clean with a non-abrasive pad.

LONGER LIFE FROM NON-STICK COATED PANS
Season with oil after each washing. Throw in 1 tbsp. oil. Wipe down all inside surfaces with a paper towel. Wipe out any excess oil with a clean paper towel so surface appears clean.

REMOVING STAINS FROM NON-STICK COATED PANS
The easiest and cheapest way is to make a solution of 2 tsp. baking soda, 1/3 cup water and 3 tbsp. ordinary liquid bleach.

Gently simmer the solution in the pan until the stains disappear. Wash with warm sudsy water, repeating this a second time.

USING SELF-ADHESIVE DECORATIVE PAPERS
If you apply them to walls, counters, etc., and then find you've got a few bubbles along the way, take a fine needle and prick the hole. Then carefully smooth out the bubble. The pinhole won't show and the bubble will be gone.

CABINET DOORS DON'T STAY CLOSED PROPERLY?
Give them a little extra power by gluing small magnets on the inside of the door and the lip. This way they are more likely to stay closed.

KIDDIES IN THE KITCHEN
If you get annoyed at your toddlers when they start emptying out the lower cabinets in an attempt to find things to play with, solve the problem by giving them their very own cabinet. Remove all items from a lower cabinet you don't use much, fill it with toys and turn it over to the baby.

DARK INTERIOR CABINETS
If you've got cabinets that are deep enough (lucky you) so that it's hard to see clearly, try this. Paint the interior in a glossy, enamel white paint. Or, buy one of those battery-operated lights which can be easily affixed to the interior wall and let the light shine in!

EXTRA SPARKLE FROM YOUR DISHWASHER
Few people think to check the filter in the bottom of the dishwasher on a regular basis. Do this weekly and clean out any trapped residue. You'll be surprised at how you get some extra sparkle out of your dishwasher with this simple little hint.

ANOTHER SIMPLE HINT FOR DISHWASHING
As much of a temptation as it is to really stack up the dishes in that machine, in the long run you do yourself a disservice. If the water can't properly spray to all of the dishes, they're not going to get clean. Wash a little less, rinse a little better and you'll have cleaner dishes.

IF YOU'VE GOT HARD WATER

It can be a real problem and obstacle to getting many, many things really clean around the house. If you've got hard water, don't stint on the detergent. You might even want to experiment with detergents to find one that is best for your machine. (Be sure to read the manufacturers directions on the box, it will probably give you some advice.)

DON'T LOSE ITEMS IN THE BOTTOM OF YOUR DISHWASHER

Instead, just put a little nylon netting or other suitable substance in the bottom of the flatware basket. It will prevent little items from slipping through.

OVEN-INNARDS

If you haven't got a self-cleaning oven, then here's a way to clean the racks without too much fuss. Put them in your dishwasher and run them through with ordinary dishwasher detergent. If they are badly encrusted with grease, soak them in the sink overnight with a good dowsing of dishwasher detergent. Rinse and run through the washer.

THE WINDOWS ON YOUR OVEN

Keeping those windows clean can really be a problem. One way to lessen the chore is to clean this part of the oven more frequently than the rest. Use ammonia or vinegar and some elbow grease. If the grease still doesn't come off, it may be that you need to unscrew the window and clean between the glass. Check manufacturers instructions before you attempt this task.

KEEP SPILLS FROM HAPPENING

When you bake in the oven, put lids on whenever possible. If baking, set utensil on a *small* tray, not much bigger than the item. This will catch some of the spills. Don't use a large amount of aluminum foil since this will interfere with the conduction of the heat.

A SIMPLE TRICK FOR REMOVING VINYL SQUARE TILES

Put your iron on hottest setting. Put a lightweight cotton towel over the tile to be removed and "iron" it for several minutes. The tile should loosen. If necessary, repeat and gently pry up from the edges.

AVOID DISCOLORATION ON YOUR KITCHEN FLOORS

If you're lucky enough to have the new no-wax floors, do not use a rubber mat or a rubber-backed rug on the floor. If you'd like to have something down to ease leg tension in the places where you do most standing in the kitchen, use a piece of carpeting remnant.

RUST STAINS IN YOUR REFRIGERATOR?

Baking soda comes to the rescue again. Use 3 tbsp. of baking soda and add enough warm water to make a thick paste. Apply and let stand for 5 minutes. Wash off with a clean sponge dipped in warm sudsy water.

MORE REFRIGERATOR AIDS

If you've got discoloration on any of the glass portion of the refrigerator, try the same formula as above. Or, use hydrogen peroxide applied with a clean, damp-dry sponge.

BEAUTIFY YOUR DISHWASHER

If you live in an area with hard water, or if small items have ever slipped through to the bottom and rusted in the dishwasher, you might want to give it a little face lift. Try this. Put 1 to 1-1/2 cups of ordinary bleach in the bottom of the washer and run through but do NOT dry. Only after this step is completed, and as a SEPARATE process, run 1-1/2 cups of cider vinegar (clear) through, using the entire cycle through dry. You're dishwasher should look and smell pretty nice.

AN EXTRA BEAUTY TIP

If you really want your dishwasher to be extra improved, after you have finished the bleach and vinegar treatment, fill both detergent cups to overflowing with baking soda and run through a wash or rinse cycle (do not bother with drying).

AN EASIER WAY TO CLEAN YOUR OVEN

This is a task that no one seems to care much for, but there are a few things you can do to make the chore a little easier. First, apply your commercial cleaner (or ammonia—it's a cheap way to accomplish the same thing) and leave on overnight. Wipe up the next morning as soon as you get up. The oven will be done before you know what happened. (Also, catch early grease problems when they happen by dowsing the area with salt to absorb the grease.)

FRESH SMELLING SINK

Just like you can use baking soda to freshen up your refrigerator, you can also use it for your sink. Pour a few heaping tablespoons down the sink. Sprinkle another heaping tablespoon on the sink scour very lightly and rinse.

RUBBER MATS FOR YOUR SINK

One way to prevent scratches in your sink is to use a rubber protector mat. To keep it looking new, let it soak for 15-20 minutes in hot water and dishwater detergent. Do this every 3-4 weeks.

CLOGGED SINK DRAINS

One way to keep clogging down is to pour leftover boiling water (from vegetables or tea) down the drain. Do this once or twice a week. If your drain is slow, first pour 1/2 cup liquid laundry detergent down the drain followed by boiling water. (If you use this method, first slowly pour in one cup boiling water, wait five minutes and then pour in another cup at a normal speed.)

SMUDGES ON YOUR REFRIGERATOR DOOR

Keep the smudge build up down by keeping a cotton or terry cloth towel hanging on the door knob. When you can see the marks, just give it a little rub and the marks will be gone. (This is a good idea because a refrig left too long is hard to clean.)

LETTERS ON YOUR REFRIGERATOR

Covering your refrigerator door with at least two sets of alphabet magnets is a great way to entertain your kids when they are in the kitchen. What most people don't know is that adults love to spell out with the letters, too.

KEEP SALT OR BAKING SODA HANDY WHEN COOKING
It's great to absorb grease and put out fires. But remember, keep it next to the stove, so you don't have to reach across a grease fire to get at it.

IF YOU'VE GOT A MESSY COOKING JOB
If you're cooking and you know there will be lots of splatters, cover the heat indicator knobs with clear plastic storage wrap. It will cut down on clean up time when you finish.

AN EASY WAY TO TREAT DISCOLORED ALUMINUM PANS
Gently simmer two - three tablespoons of cream of tartar in water in the pot for 30 minutes. The discoloration should be gone.

BURNED FOOD IN A POT OR PAN
If you can do something about it right away, try this. Fill the utensil with *hot* water to cover the burned food. Add a squirt of dishwashing liquid and gently simmer for 15-30 minutes, depending upon the severity of the burned particles.

GLASS BAKING DISHES WITH BAKED ON FOOD
If you've got glass baking dishes that *used* to shine, but now are dull and lifeless because of encrusted spills that you can't even begin to get off, try this. Clean with a commercial oven cleaner. Then wash as usual.

A TIP FOR STORING COATED PANS
Never stack them without some kind of protection. Put in an old *plastic* lid or a paper towel to separate it from the next utensil. This will prevent unnecessary scratching and lengthen the life of the pan.

IF YOU'VE GOT A BAD SINK STAIN

Don't scrub it with a strong abrasive (and ruin the finish), instead bleach them or use a little baking soda and a nylon scrub brush.

PRETTYING UP YOUR SINK AREA

If your sink does not face a window or other attractive area, pay some special attention to it. Think about how many hours you spend at that sink. And then think of something nice you could put there. Perhaps it's a favorite picture. Or a nice mirror to reflect what's going on behind you. But don't leave the area blank—you have too many hours up against that wall!

EASE FATIGUE AT THE SINK

Try putting a piece of old carpeting down. Or a nice thick rubber mat. It will help to ease some of the tension from standing.

IF YOU EVER BURN YOUR COUNTERTOP

It's not uncommon to have an unsightly scorch on a laminated sink top. If it ever happens to you, turn that space into some kind of work area. If you're lucky enough to be handy, you can actually cut out the area and replace it with butcherblocking. Or put a wooden cutting board over the area. Or, if it's out of the way, try decorative tiles, or even a decorative appliqué.

GETTING AROUND EASIER IN YOUR FREEZER

If you've every been stuck with "routing" around in the freezer, looking for goods you know must be in there somewhere, try making up a list of items, by shelf. Put the list in a little freezer bag and tape it to the shelf it goes with, in the freezer. As you add items, just throw in another little piece of paper into the plastic bag. Or cross them out as you use them. Then, when you want something, just look through the clear bags. You'll be able to spot what shelf the item is on, and go right for it.

ORGANIZING A CHEST-TYPE FREEZER

Take sturdy shopping bags (best with handles) and stack the food (best by category) in the bags. Then drop the bags in the freezer. Then, when you want something, just lift the bag out by its handles. P.S. I'ts even more efficient to "inventory" the contents of each bag on the outside of the bag, or using clear baggies as noted above.

USING YOUR OVEN RACK
If you're baking and it needs to cool on a rack, use the extra one from your oven. It will give you plenty of space.

DO YOUR DISHWASHER RACKS STICK?
If so, there are a few things you can do. First, try a scrub down with a steel wool soap pad. Pay special attention to the metal tracks, because that's usually where the problem lies. If they are still sticking after that, scour the racks and tracks with cider vinegar, applied directly. Then run over the whole area once again with the steel wool soap pad.

KEEP YOUR DISH CLEANING UP TO DATE
If you've got a dishwasher that's not completely full, use the rest of the space to run through a few dishes that you don't use too often that are gathering dust. That way when you want to use them, they will be clean and ready to go.

IF YOU NEED TO DEFROST YOUR REFRIGERATOR
Do the work with a pair of clean garden gloves or even the cooking "mittens" (although the latter tends to be a little bulky). You'll be able to work faster without worry of "freezer burns".

AN EXTRA TRICK TO MAKE DEFROSTING FREEZERS EASIER
Wax paper, used as a shelf liner in the freezer, will go a long ways towards speeding up the defrosting process the next time you've got to do it. Just pull out the paper and watch most of the caked up ice go with it!

CLEANING ALUMINUM STOVE TOPS
If you'd like your stove top to sparkle, take 3 tbsp. of cream of tartar. Add enough water to make a paste that's easily spreadable. Spread it on, wait five minutes and wipe clean with a sponge.

IF YOUR CERAMIC STOVE TOP IS DISCOLORED...

Now that's easy. Dip a clean sponge into some white cider vinegar and wipe it clean. The discoloration should come right up. If necessary, repeat.

VINEGAR THE CURE-ALL

It can be used for so many things, from discolorations to general, all-purpose cleaning. Put a little extra sparkle in your chrome and wipe it down with cider vinegar.

STOVE CLEAN UP CAN BE EASIER

Keep a stack of disposable pie tins by the stove. When you're frying or boiling something that's likely to splatter, cover burners not in use with the pie tins. Clean up will be a lot easier.

IF YOU LOSE FOOD BETWEEN COUNTERS

Sometimes there is a small space between refrigerator or stove and counters. Counteract by filling in with aluminum stripping or even some weather stripping.

KEEP MILDEW DOWN

If you find a lot of mildew in your kitchen, it might just be because of the humidity level. Air the kitchen twice a day. If you have an exhaust fan you can run that twice a day instead of leaving doors and windows open.

TILE COUNTERS GET STAINED

If you get mildew or other stains in the grout between your tiles, rectify the situation by applying laundry bleach. Soak a paper towel or small sponge with bleach and leave for several hours. Wipe dry with a small sponge and then paper towel dry.

HARD WATER AND YOUR TILES

If you find you've got mineral deposits on your tiles from the hard water, soak the area with paper towels that have been wetted with cider vinegar. Leave for several hours. Wipe dry with a sponge and paper towel dry.

CLEANING YOUR MICROWAVE

Cover over the soiled area with two sheets of paper toweling which have been soaked in water. Turn the oven on medium for 20 seconds. Wipe up the soiled area when the oven has cooled off.

STORE SINK SOAP ATOP A SPONGE
If you do, you'll have less mess to clean up, you'll have plenty of soap suds whenever you need them, and the soap will stay put.

RUBBER BOTTOMED UTENSILS
If you have utensils, such as a toaster or blender, that leave little black marks on your counter from the rubber tips, try gluing a little felt to the bottom and you won't have any more marks. This felt can easily be replaced on a periodic basis.

COFFEE FILTERS
Have you ever gone to make coffee for the family only to discover that you've run out of filters? Use a heavy duty paper napkin instead. Or, barring that, use a double thickness of an ordinary paper napkin.

CLEANING THAT FILTER OVER THE STOVE
Have you ever looked up and been totally dismayed at the grease build up on these filters? Sometimes it seems that the only alternative is to throw it away. Not so. Pop it into your dishwasher and clean with your other dishes. You'll be amazed at the results. Do this on a regular basis and you'll never have any grease build up.

FIXING CHIPPED PORCELAIN
You can buy kits to do just this. They even have colored ones to match your needs. Or, add a little food coloring to a neutral color and mix your own.

SHINING STAINLESS STEEL FLATWARE
If you're disappointed with the dull lustre that has accumulated on your flatware, try soaking all of it in a basin of warm water mixed with 1 cup of cider vinegar. Soak for 10-15 minutes, rinse thoroughly in warm water, wash quickly in sudsy, warm water and dry. It should be sparkling with no vinegar odor.

STORING SHARP KNIVES

Find yourself an attractive container that you'd like to keep out on the countr that's also deep enough to hold your knives. Then fill it half full with rice. Plunge your knives into the rice and they'll stay firm and be attractively displayed.

CLEANING BLENDER BLADES

Next time you've used the blender, throw in a few cubes of ice and turn blender on until ice is crushed. This will nicely clean off deposits which are hard to get at. P.S. You can also try this trick with your kitchen sink disposal unit. The ice will clean off any dried on refuse.

BRUSH YOUR CAN OPENER!

If your can opener has a food build up on the blades, try this. First disconnect it. Then dip a toothbrush into warm, sudsy water and brush the blades. Rinse brush and dip into warm, clear water and rinse in the same manner.

Collectibles and Decorative ACCESSORIES

INTRODUCTION FOR COLLECTIBLES & DECORATIVE ACCESSORIES

You can have the most beautiful carpeting or wood floors, and the finest furniture, yet if your house is bare of the "extras"— collectibles you've amassed lovingly through the years or the prized decorative accessories, it will not feel furnished. However, these small items are just the worst collectors of dust in your home. They are open invitations to the grime and dirt in the air.

Since they are made of such a variety of substances, you must have the special knowledge of exactly how to clean each one. In this chapter on household accessories, we give you everything from tips on working with floral arrangements to how to make candles last longer. We offer cleaning suggestions on artificial flowers, paintings, and pewter bowls. We discuss how to care for silver, copper, gold, bronze, brass, pewter, platinum, etc. We even tell you how to repair a favorite leaking vase. This chapter will help you care for all your household accessories easily and quickly, and you'll be proud of that special touch, fine looking accessories add to any decor.

HERE'S A WAY TO KEEP YOUR FLOWERS OR LARGE LEAVES IN PLACE ONCE YOU HAVE COMPLETED AN ARRANGEMENT.
Take a piece of cardboard or even some foam rubber, and cut a shape to fit the neck of your vase. Then use a loose-leaf hole puncher to punch several holes. You can then string your flower stems though the holes and your flowers will be separated as you wish, and stay in place.

TRY THIS WAY TO AVOID CUTTING YOUR FINGERS AND ARMS WHEN YOU WORK WITH ROSES THAT HAVE THORNS.
Use a large pair of tweezers to handle the roses as much as possible. Also, save an old pair of gloves which you no longer need and use them for this purpose.

IF YOU WANT COLORFUL DAISIES, HERE'S AN EASY WAY TO TIE YOUR FLOWERS INTO YOUR DECORATIVE COLOR SCHEME.

First, take a sharp knife and slice across the stems at a 45 degree angle. Then take approximately 2 ounces of food coloring and mix it with 1/3 cup of warm water. Then place the stems of the daisies in the dye solution, propping them against a solid backing. Allow them to steep in the solution for 5 to 6 hours. Then remove your newly coordinated daisies!

KEEP CUTTING BACK AT THOSE STEMS TO LENGTHEN THE LIFE OF YOUR FLOWERS!

Snip a small amount of the stems of your floral arrangements every day. This will allow your flowers to keep absorbing the water and thus prolong their life. Maintain the angle of the stem each day.

WHENEVER YOU RECEIVE A GIFT OF FLOWERS, BE SURE TO PUT THEM IN FRESH WATER.

Many people make the mistake of thinking that just because flowers have arrived from a florist, that they are all set for a day or two. Nothing is further from the truth. During the time that they travel, it is virtually impossible to ensure that they have enough water. So be sure to check that the stems are cut at an angle and the flowers are set in cool, fresh water.

TRY THIS TRICK BEFORE DECIDING THAT YOUR FLOWERS ARE READY FOR THE REFUSE HEAP.

Sometimes you can revive flowers that appear to be drooping by clearing a space in your refrigerator and placing the flowers there for about 45 minutes. It is worth a try to give those flowers one last chance!

IF A FEW FLOWERS IN YOUR ARRANGEMENT ARE DROOPY, DOES THAT MEAN YOU HAVE TO DISCARD ALL OF THEM?

Nothing looks worse than a flower arrangement that is only half alive. When the flowers show signs of drooping, remove those that are dying and replace with some compatible flowers or even some green leaves. There's no need to throw out the entire arrangement if only part is fading.

IF YOUR CANDLES ARE ALWAYS BURNING DOWN TOO FAST, HERE'S A WAY TO KEEP THEM GOING.

First, place your candle in the refrigerator for approximately one hour. Then transfer to the freezer for about 45 minutes. The candle will burn at a slower rate and you'll get less of those annoying drippings as well.

HAS YOUR FAVORITE SILVER CANDLE HOLDER BECOME COVERED OVER WITH WAX DRIPPINGS? THIS IS A SIMPLE WAY TO CORRECT THE SITUATION.

First, gently peel off the wax that is easily removable. Then, place the candlestick or holder on a piece of tin foil in the freezer compartment of your refrigerator. In about two hours, the candle will be easy to work with and you'll be able to peel off the wax in no time.

TRY THIS FOR CLEANING THE FRAMES OF YOUR PAINTINGS.

Take a soft cleaning cloth and dampen it with turpentine. Be careful not to have the turpentine too soaking wet. Then clean the frame with the treated cloth. Allow to dry thoroughly—this may take two or three days. Do not handle during the drying period. You'll have a frame that is clean and new looking.

WANT AN EASY WAY TO CLEAN YOUR CRYSTAL CHANDELIER? THIS DOES THE TRICK!

Take a plastic cup that is taller than the height of your largest chandelier crystal. Fill with a solution of 1/4 cup alcohol and 3/4 cup water. Then simply dip each crystal pendant in the cup and your chandelier will be sparkling. Be sure to cover your floor area under the chandelier before starting to work.

IF YOUR ARTIFICIAL FLOWERS ARE BEGINNING TO LOOK GRIMY, SOME ORDINARY HOUSEHOLD SALT WILL HELP MAKE THEM CLEAN AGAIN.

Place approximately 6 tablespoons of salt in a plastic bag, and add your flowers. Then shake up and down and from side to side quite firmly. Remove the flowers, which should be considerably cleaner, for the salt will absorb the dirt.

THIS EASY WAY OF CLEANING WAX OFF YOUR SILVER CANDLESTICK REALLY WORKS!
Place the candlestick in your kitchen sink and fill with the hottest water available. The hotter the better. Soak for approximately 5 minutes. And then all you need do is dry it off with a paper towel, and your candlestick will be free of wax.

IT MAY SOUND STRANGE, BUT THIS REALLY WORKS TO CLEAN YOUR PEWTER BOWLS OR OTHER ACCESSORIES MADE OF PEWTER.
Take a few leaves of cabbage and rub them over the item. The chemical action works wonders with pewter.

IF YOU NEED TO CLEAN A VASE THAT HAS A VERY NARROW NECK, TRY THIS.
First, rinse the vase out with warm water. Next, add some bathroom cleaner or even the cleaner you use for the toilet bowl, along with a bit of water. Allow this to stand for approximately 10 to 15 minutes, and then place your hand over the neck of the vase and shake gently. Then rinse thoroughly and your vase will be clean inside.

IF YOUR FAVORITE VASE HAS STARTED TO LEAK, YOU CAN REPAIR IT WITH THIS EASY SOLUTION.
Take some liquid paraffin and generously coat the inside of the vase. Allow the paraffin to harden overnight. This will form a plug for the vase and it should last a long time.

IF YOUR PICTURES REFUSE TO HANG STRAIGHT, THIS SHOULD "STRAIGHTEN" THE SITUATION.
Take some masking tape and carefully wind it around the picture wire, working it about 2-1/2 inches either side of the center. When you rehang your picture, you'll be pleased at the results.

IF YOUR PICTURED FRAMES ARE UNFINISHED AND YOU ARE READY TO TURN THEM INTO A "WOOD" LOOK, HERE'S HOW TO GET A WALNUT-LIKE FINISH.

Take some dark brown shoe polish in liquid form and apply a coating to the frame. Allow to dry thoroughly, and then use another coat. When this has dried, wax with paste wax, and you'll have a frame that looks like walnut.

BEFORE HANGING A NEW PICTURE, USE THIS TECHNIQUE TO PREVENT PLASTER HOLES IN YOUR WALL.

Mark the place where you will be hammering the nail with a pencil. A small circle will do. Then, place a piece of transparent tape over the area, and hammer your nail through the tape. This will prevent those unsightly holes in the wall.

IF YOUR FAVORITE PAINTING IS NOT HANGING STRAIGHT, TRY THIS.

Go to your local hardware store and get some mounting squares. These are adhesive-backed squares. Then simply press one on each corner of your picture backing and when you press your picture in place on the wall, it will be straight.

BE SURE NEVER TO USE A CLOTH ON YOUR FINE PAINTINGS. IT WILL DAMAGE THE FINISH.

Instead, use the upholstery brush attachment on your vacuum cleaner and gently clean the surface of the painting.

TO ENSURE THAT NO LIQUID CLEANSER RUNS UNDER THE GLASS OF YOUR PAINTINGS, TRY THIS SUBSTITUTE.

Take the tissue that is used to clean a camera lense, and carefully clean the glass of your picture. There'll be no chance of water damage.

KEEP YOUR PLEATED LAMPSHADE CLEAN THE EASY WAY!

Take a cosmetic brush, the kind that is used to apply face powder, and brush the shade with that. It will do wonders!

OR USE THE COMMON HAIR DRYER.

Take your hair blow dryer and turn it on the lowest setting. Then move it to remove any dust that is lodged in the pleats of your lampshade.

COLLECT YOUR KNICKKNACKS TO SAVE TIME IN CLEANING.

Instead of laboriously cleaning each and every knickknack separately, simply gather a group of them and place them in the kitchen sink on a rubber mat. Immerse them in a solution of mild detergent and lukewarm water. Then rinse carefully and use your hand-held hair dryer to blow dry. All you'll have to do is put them back in place!

IF YOU HAVE A COLLECTIBLE THAT IS VERY DELICATE AND HAS HARD-TO-REACH SPOTS, TRY A LITTLE ARTISTIC CLEANING!

Get an artist's brush that has a small long brush. Usually, these have handles long enough so that you can reach all those hard-to-get places with ease.

IF YOU USE A LIQUID GLASS CLEANER ON YOUR PICTURE FRAMES, NEVER SPRAY IT DIRECTLY ON THE GLASS.

Spraying cleaner on the glass may lead to liquid seepage that will damage your artwork. So, instead, spray the liquid directly onto your cleaning cloth. Be sure it is just damp, and not soaking wet. Then, carefully clean the glass and you'll have sparkle without the chance of ruining the art.

DON'T LET YOUR PEWTER BOWLS OR FLATWARE BUILD UP STAINS. EARLY CARE AFTER USE IS IMPORTANT.

Never allow your pewter accessories to sit around after they have been used. They can gather stains or become pitted so easily. So be sure to wash them as quickly as possible.

ANOTHER TIP FOR PEWTER—ONE THAT WILL SAVE YOU TIME.

Although it may seem strange, pewter objects benefit from use.

The ones that are used on a regular basis actually keep their polish better than those that simply sit around. So—use your pewter more frequently and you'll work less at polishing it.

A WARNING—DON'T LET YOUR PEWTER BOWLS SIT ON A HOT STOVE.

Pewter is very susceptible to heat—and so you should never allow your pewter bowls or plates to be close to a hot stove or oven. It is even advisable not to serve foods that are piping hot in them.

PEWTER IS VERY EASY TO CARE FOR—YOU DON'T NEED ANYTHING SPECIAL TO KEEP IT IN GOOD SHAPE.

The best way to wash pewter is with a mild liquid detergent in a solution of lukewarm water. It does not need special pewter cleaner the way that brass or copper does.

SINCE COPPER TENDS TO DISCOLOR, TRY THIS TRICK TO KEEP YOUR COPPER IN GOOD SHAPE.

First, clean your copper objects with a product that has an acid base. Then add some mild soap to a tub of warm water and dip the objects in the solution. Your copper will retain its "coppery" finish.

SINCE COPPER TENDS TO TARNISH EASILY, HERE'S A TIP THAT WILL MAKE THIS PROCESS SLOW DOWN.

Most hardware stores carry a special polish for copper that is designed to prevent tarnishing. These polishes have a special chemical that is just for this purpose. Keep a can on hand for your special copper bowls and other decorative objects.

DON'T WAIT UNTIL YOUR COPPER BOWLS ARE TARNISHED TO CLEAN THEM.

It is much easier to keep copper looking well if you clean your copper objects routinely. Don't wait until they are dirty. Use a clean cloth and then some copper polish to ensure your copper staying bright and shiny.

FOR THOSE PRECIOUS DECORATIVE OBJECTS MADE OF GOLD, SOME GENTLE CARE WILL KEEP THEM LOOKING BRILLIANT.

On a regular basis, you should clean your gold objects with a damp cleaning cloth, and then buff them gently until they are dry to get that luster back. If the gold surface looks like it is dulling, try a metal polish to remedy this.

IF YOUR ANDIRONS HAVE BECOME STAINED AND BLACK, TRY THIS EASY WAY TO GET THEM SHINING AGAIN.

Take some very fine steel wool, the finest grade you can find, and apply some cooking oil to the andirons. Be sure not to scrub too hard or you'll wear away the finish. Then, you can use your regular brass polish to get the andirons back to their shining glory.

DON'T THINK THAT RUBBING YOUR BRONZE DECORATIVE OBJECTS AS HARD AS YOU CAN WILL CLEAN THEM BETTER. IT CAN ACTUALLY DAMAGE YOUR BRONZE.

Some bronze objects are not bronze through and through, but have only a bronze coating. If you rub too heavily on these, you can actually rub off the bronze coating after a period of time. So a little caution is advisable. Rub your bronze gently.

IF THE LACQUER FINISH ON YOUR BRONZE STATUE IS WEARING OFF, DON'T TRY TO REPAIR IT YOURSELF.

The lacquer on a bronze piece is quite delicate—and really needs professional care if it has begun to crack. Take it to a fine restorer or even a jeweler to have the surface professionally repaired.

IF YOUR BRONZE OBJECTS HAVE ACQUIRED A DIRTY FILM, HERE'S HOW TO RESTORE THEM TO THEIR ORIGINAL STATE.

Take a mild soap solution and dip the bronze object in it. Then dry with a soft clean cloth and buff gently. Your bronze collectible will be clean and glowing.

85

BRASS ACCESSORIES NEED REGULAR CARE. FOLLOW THIS HINT AND YOUR BRASS WILL STAY LOOKING BEAUTIFUL FOR YEARS.
Be sure to dust your brass objects regularly, particularly those that have been lacquered. From time to time, you can go over them with a damp cleaning cloth, but be sure that the cloth is barely damp.

CHECK YOUR BRASS FIRST—BE SURE THAT IT IS NOT LACQUERED BEFORE USING A BRASS CLEANER.
A brass cleaner is wonderful, but only for brass which has not been lacquered. Don't use it on lacquered pieces, for you'll eat through the finish.

IF YOUR BRASS OBJECTS CANNOT BE PLACED IN WATER, HERE'S HOW TO KEEP THEM CLEAN.
Get a cloth that has been given special treatment at your local hardware store. Then you can polish your brass accessory with the cloth. If the directions state not to soak in water, be very sure to follow them. More than once a beloved decoration has been ruined by immersing it in water.

IF YOUR LACQUERED BRASS OBJECTS ARE PEELING AND THE LACQUER HAS BEGUN TO COME LOOSE, HERE'S HOW TO TREAT THEM.
You have no choice but to remove the lacquer. Use a solution of 1 gallon of water to 2/3 of a cup baking soda. When the article is placed in the water, leave it for an hour. Then peel the lacquer.

IF YOU DECIDE TO TAKE A SHORTCUT AND POP YOUR PEWTER BOWLS INTO THE DISHWASHER, HEED THIS WARNING.
NEVER, NEVER put pewter objects in your dishwasher. Pewter has a tendency to discolor markedly when it goes through a dishwasher process.

IF YOUR PEWTER HAS SOME SUBSTANCES THAT HAVE "GOOKED" ONTO THE SURFACE, DON'T MAKE THIS MISTAKE.
One of the common mistakes people make with pewter, because

it appears so hardy, is to use steel wool or a harsh cleanser on it. This will mar the surface of the pewter, and so, whatever you do, treat your pewter with care.

PEWTER IS SUSCEPTIBLE TO CERTAIN FOODS, SO BEWARE OF THESE.

If you have used a pewter object as a salt cellar or a container for your salad dressing, be very careful. These are substances that should be removed from pewter as quickly as possible. In fact, we advise that you do not use them for this purpose if you can help it.

IF YOU RUN YOUR SILVER THROUGH THE DISHWASHER, BE VERY CAREFUL THAT IT DOES NOT TOUCH ANYTHING ELSE.

Silver can be ruined in the dishwasher if it touches other objects during the washing cycle. So keep your silver apart from the balance of your dishwasher load, in a separate area or compartment.

WHEN YOU DECIDE TO POLISH YOUR SILVER, DON'T JUST TAKE OUT THE POLISH AND ATTACK IT!

Before using silver polish on your fine silver objects, it is advisable to wash it first in some warm soapy water. Then rinse thoroughly and dry before polishing.

IF YOUR SILVER HAS A LOT OF CARVING, AND IS REALLY DIFFICULT TO GET POLISHED, TRY THIS OLD TRICK!

You can take an old toothbrush and use it to help you get to those difficult patterns. Be sure that the toothbrush is a very soft one so that it doesn't wear the silver. There are specially made silver brushes that do the same job, but they are usually more expensive than your "improvised" brush.

AFTER CLEANING YOUR SILVER, BE SURE TO GET ALL THE POLISH OFF.

Nothing dulls old silver more than a coating of polish that gets left on when you finish cleaning it. After using your polish, rinse your silver in some warm water and dry with a clean soft towel.

Finish the job right! And to top it off, buff with a soft dry cloth for that extra shine!

IF YOU HAVE SILVER THAT IS ONLY FOR DECORATIVE USE, SAVE YOURSELF SOME WORK WITH THIS EASY PROCESS.

Take the silver to your local jeweler and ask him to put a coating of lacquer over it. This will prevent the ordinary amount of tarnish from developing and save you a lot of work!

WHEN CLEANING SILVER ORNAMENTAL OBJECTS, BE CAREFUL IF YOUR OBJECTS ARE PLATED RATHER THAN STERLING.

The plating on silver objects is only a thin layer of silver over a base metal. Thus, when you clean, you are actually wearing down the silver coating. So—be more careful when you clean silver plate to ensure that the plating will remain in place for a long time.

IF YOU THINK THAT "SAVING" YOUR SILVER OBJECTS WILL KEEP THEM CLEAN, THEN YOU ARE WRONG!

Actually, using silver objects on a regular basis will help to reduce the amount of tarnish that they collect. We recommend that you use your silver objects at least every 2 weeks in order to cut down the amount of work you will have to do on upkeep.

IF THERE IS SILVER THAT YOU RARELY USE, IT IS BEST TO STORE IT IN SPECIAL CHESTS.

If you have silver that you rarely use, don't let it simply sit around in your regular silver drawer. There are a large variety of chests, or even rolls, that are designed especially for silver. These will keep your silver from tarnishing in between uses. An investment well worth the work it will save you!

IF YOU ARE FORTUNATE ENOUGH TO OWN ANY OBJECTS OF PLATINUM, THAT RARE AND PRECIOUS METAL, BE SURE TO TREAT IT WITH THE CARE THAT IT DESERVES. HERE'S HOW TO KEEP IT CLEAN.

Use a soft cloth regularly to remove any smudges on the surface.

This should do the job and keep your platinum looking wonderful. However, if you forget to care for it regularly, and it becomes dirty, then use a cloth that has been dipped in a solution of mild soap and lukewarm water and wipe the object carefully.

ANOTHER WAY TO CLEAN YOUR PLATINUM OBJECTS IS THE BASIS OF THIS SIMPLE HINT.

Use some baking soda straight from the box on a soft clean cloth. Before you know it, the platinum will be bright and shiny once more.

IF YOUR PLATINUM HAS BECOME GREASY OR STICKY, YOU WILL HAVE TO RESORT TO THIS METHOD TO GET IT BACK TO NORMAL.

Make a solution of liquid dishwashing detergent or the mildest detergent you can find—about a capful to a half gallon of water. Then dip your object in the suds for a minute or two, and rinse in clear, warm water buffing with a clean soft chamois cloth to restore that wonderful shine.

WHEN YOU USE SILVER AS SERVING CONTAINERS, BEAR THESE DIFFICULT SUBSTANCES IN MIND.

Eggs, or any other substance with a high degree of sulphur should never be allowed to stay on silver for very long, because it will stain your silver. Salt causes the same problem. So be very careful of what you serve in your silver.

WHEN YOU POLISH YOUR SILVER AND NEED TO PROTECT YOUR HANDS, GO PLASTIC!

Admittedly, it is difficult to polish silver because you want to protect your hands from the polish. However, whatever you do, do not use rubber gloves for this. This is because rubber tends to act to tarnish the silver—the very thing you are trying to prevent. Another solution is to use plastic gloves, the kind that are disposable. They will serve the same purpose, but keep your hard work from being useless.

WHEN YOU ARE READY TO CLEAN YOUR PORCELAIN OBJECTS, DON'T ATTACK THEM WITH TOO MUCH VIGOR!

Although you may want to do the best cleaning job possible, remember that porcelain is a very fragile and delicate material. So be sure to handle your porcelain very carefully in the cleaning process.

A GOOD, SOFT CLEANING CLOTH WILL GO A LONG WAY WITH PORCELAIN.

If you do it regularly, a thorough dusting with a soft cleaning cloth will be all that your porcelain articles will require.

IF YOUR PORCELAIN HAS GOTTEN DIRTY, HERE'S THE WAY TO CLEAN IT.

Porcelain objects should be treated with great care when cleaning. So, if you must wash them, use lukewarm water and a very mild soap solution. Then soak the porcelain for a few minutes, gently running a soft wet cloth over the pieces. Be sure never to use very hot water.

TRY THIS TRICK TO AVOID BREAKING PORCELAIN WHEN CLEANING IN YOUR SINK.

Take a regular kitchen towel or old piece of flannel clothing and place it at the bottom of the sink. If you have the type of faucet that rotates around, you might also want to pad this in order to prevent any possible breakage.

EVEN IF YOUR PORCELAIN LOOKS VERY DIRTY. DON'T EVER USE STEEL WOOL.

Porcelain should be treated very gently, and even if very dirty, rely on gentle soap and water. Never, never use an abrasive steel wool or abrasive cleaner on it.

DON'T PUT YOUR IVORY IN THE DARK!

Ivory is one substance which needs a supply of light—if you keep it in a dark spot, it tends to yellow. So be sure to give your precious ivory collectibles a bright spot.

BE CAREFUL WITH IVORY GROUPINGS—DON'T GET THEM IN THE WATER.

If you have a group of ivory objects that have been bound together, often cement is used. So be careful never to put them in water for any long period or you may loosen the cement.

IF YOU HAVE IVORY CUTLERY, DON'T USE SHORT-CUTS.

Even though it may be tempting, never put ivory cutlery into your dishwasher. It can really destroy the ivory. This goes for cutlery that has ivory handles or even your ivory letter opener.

TRY THIS TO COUNTERACT YELLOWED IVORY.

If your favorite ivory object has started to turn yellow, you can retard this process by taking half a lemon, rubbing it in some salt, and then running it over your ivory object. The lemon will work on the yellow, and, after it is dry, just take a soft cloth that has been dampened with some lukewarm water and rub to give it a bright finish.

DON'T WASH YOUR JADE.

Jade does not require much care, and it is not advisable to wash it. Simply dusting it with a chamois cloth should do the job, and if it doesn't, use a damp cloth and then a dry one.

PORCELAIN VALUABLES MEAN THAT YOU CANNOT TAKE THE SHORT WAY OUT.

Porcelain is very subject to any sudden change in temperature, so don't ever make the mistake of thinking that you can put your porcelain objects in the dishwasher. Exposing porcelain to the high temperatures might ruin the glaze.

TREAT YOUR ORNAMENTAL GLASS CAREFULLY— IT MEANS A BIT MORE WORK, BUT IT WILL SAVE YOU POTENTIAL BREAKAGE.

Fine ornamental glass is best treated by hand washing, particularly if there is any gold or silver trim on the glassware. A little extra work will mean years more of life for your valued glass objects.

WHEN WASHING GLASS BY HAND, TAKE EVERY PRE-CAUTION TO ENSURE THAT THERE IS NO BREAKAGE. When you are ready to wash your glassware, use a towel or rubber mat on the sink bottom to prevent breakage.

WALLS, WINDOWS and CEILINGS

INTRODUCTION FOR WINDOWS, WALLS, AND CEILINGS

Nothing tells more about a house than the condition of those true essentials—windows, walls, and ceilings. For they provide the basis on which all other housekeeping elements are displayed. You can have the most beautiful furniture and the most costly decorative accessories in your home, but if your windows are dull and dirty, your walls full of grime or crayon marks and your ceilings unsightly, none of your wonderful possessions will be displayed to advantage.

Your house or apartment can really become a beautiful home with the added personal touches this chapter will help you to provide to your interior. Good maintenance of walls, windows, and ceilings is essential to the life of any abode, from efficiency units to large family dwellings.

We invite you to see how easily and inexpensively you can do most minor and many major tasks. We've assembled a host of tips on everything from simple carpentry to how to clean your wallpaper to how to remove ceiling stains. Join the many others who in this day and age have found it convenient and economical to do their own handywork, and make your house a showplace with the least effort possible.

EMBARASSED BY UGLY GREASE STAINS ON YOUR CEILINGS?

Here's two ways to remove them: 1) Try rubbing the stain with a laundry starch cube or an art gum eraser; or 2) If you are chemically minded, mix a solution of magnesium and carbon tetrachloride, apply to stain, let dry overnight, and brush off. Repeat if necessary.

WANT TO CLEAN YOUR WALLPAPER WITHOUT WASHING IT AWAY?

First go over it with a soft cloth or a whisk broom to remove excess dust. Then mix up a batch of 1/2 cup soap flakes, 2 tablespoons washing soda, and 2 cups hot water. Mix in a blender. Let cool and mix again. Using a soft sponge, apply thick suds to a very small area (you want to test the area), using as little water as possible. Rub lightly, and then use a second clean sponge to rinse. Blot dry with clean cloth.

CLEANING YOUR LIVING ROOM WALLS CAN BE EASY AND INEXPENSIVE.

Just mix up a solution of 1/2 cup ammonia, 1/2 cup white vinegar, 1/4 cup borax and one gallon of warm water. Be sure to test a small area before applying cleaning solution in a highly visible area.

FINGERPRINTS AND I JUST WASHED THAT WALL!

To spot clean annoying fingerprints, use plain water and a soft sponge. Go over the prints with light up and down strokes, and then dry in the same way with a soft cloth.

COMB THAT NAIL INTO PLACE!

If you've got butterfingers like so many people when it comes to hammering, try this simple trick. Take an old comb and add it to your tool box. The next time you're hammering, just wedge the tack or nail into the teeth of the comb. You'll be able to accurately hammer without stinging or bruising a finger.

LOOKING FOR STUDS?

Some people have a real knack for tapping a wall and telling sound differences and identifying the exact location of this very important wall support. If you're not as sensitive, and need to know where one of these is—or isn't—here are a few ways to locate them. First, you can look for "evidence" in the base-boards. Often, you'll find that the baseboard has been nailed into the stud. The nails are your evidence. If someone has been such a craftsperson that the nails are covered over and painted, seek out the electric outlets in the room. They are NEVER located in studs. Generally, they are located to one side or the other of a stud. If you remove the outlet cover, you can often "peek" into the wall and see the stud.

MORE WAYS TO LOCATE WALL STUDS

If you really can't find a stud on your own, try using an inexpensive tool called a stud locator. You can pick them up in any hardware store. The principle of how it works is based on metal. There's a magnet in the tool which is attracted to the metal in the nails. Move it across the wall and presto! you'll locate the stud. Once you've found one stud, you'll find the others at regular intervals, generally 24 inches apart.

CLEANING WINDOWS IS A *TWO PERSON* JOB.

First, find a partner. One person should work on the inside, while the other works on the outside. This way, you can avoid streaking.—Mix a simple solution of 2 tablespoons of ammonia or alcohol or vinegar per quart of warm water, and fill a spray bottle. To wash the windows, use a sponge and then wipe across the window with either newspaper or a chamois cloth.

DID YOU KNOW THAT YOU CAN MAKE WINDOW CLEANER THAT IS JUST AS GOOD AS THE BLUE STUFF YOU BUY IN THE STORES?

If you must have blue window cleaner, just add a little blue food coloring to a solution of 2 parts ammonia and 1 part distilled water. Presto! You have window cleaner just as good as most of the name brands.

DON'T LET THE BUGS GET YOU DOWN

Have you ever been frustrated to see a nice fat fly land right in your fresh outdoor painting efforts. Keep them away by including a little bug repellent in the paint.

BEAUTY TREATMENT FOR YOUR PAINT BRUSH

Give you paint brush a good combing before you begin to paint. It will remove loose bristles and you won't have to pick them out of your painted walls and ceilings.

EFFICIENT RECORD KEEPING

Who ever thought of recording the paint usage and colors, but how many times have you ever wished you'd done it. Even if you have, how many times has the record been lost when you went to find it. Try this hint for easy future reference. On the inside of a closet wall, write down the paint manufacturer, the color(s) used, and the amount of paint for each room. When you go to re-paint, you'll have a handy record.

PROTECT CARPETING WHEN PAINTING BASEBOARDS
Press down the carpeting with a sturdy piece of cardboard to keep paint from touching the carpet. You'll have a clean edge and a disposable paint protector.

LOOSE WALLPAPER CAN BE FIXED
Many people think that once wallpaper begins to come loose, that it's a hopeless case. That's simply not true. Ordinary glues such as rubber cement and many of the new "crazies" are very good at adhering paper back to the wall. The secret is not to wait. As soon as you see paper loosen, fix it immediately. Loose paper is likely to tear, and that's when the problems begin.

IF YOU THINK CONTACT PAPER CAN'T BE RE-MOVED...
Pry up a corner and put your hairdryer on heat. Direct it into the corner and watch the paper start to lift.

GET THE STICK OUT OF THE CONTACT PAPER
If you're left with a lot of sticky substance on the surface once you've removed the paper, any ordinary spot remover will do. Or, spot some Benzine on the area to soften the stickum. Then some glass cleaner should get rid of the rest.

HIGH CEILINGS SOMETIMES PRESENT A PROBLEM FOR WORKING WITH STANDARD SIZE MATERIALS
Although high ceiling rooms are very elegant, they can also be expensive to fix up if you plan to do anything other than paint. That's because the surfaces are greater than the standard eight foot sizes. But there is a lovely, and inexpensive way around it. The next time you're redecorating, include some chair rail molding. That way you can use standard lengths and there will be no patching. Or, another way around it is to use crown molding at

the top. Run the materials from bottom to top and "piece" with the crown molding.

GRIT ON YOUR SILLS
If you live in the city, you're very likely to find that pollution levels increase tremendously in the winter months, thus causing a build up of grit on your sills. Eventually this will find its way into all parts of your home. To keep dirt down, keep the grit level down. Make it your purpose to vacuum up the grit each day. One of those new hand held vacuumers will make the job go a lot faster.

MOISTURE BETWEEN GLASS
For those of you who have double insulated window panes, you're likely to find that the seal breaks at some point during the life of the window and that it will be necessary to do something about it. If this occurs after the guaranty is over, it can be suctioned out and re-sealed at very little expense. And your window will look as good as new. Don't let someone sell you a new window replacement unless the glass is broken.

WAX YOUR WINDOWS
If you're having trouble with the "glide" on your windows, try a little ordinary household wax or paraffin. Just apply it to the track and you'll find it's enough lubrication to get the windows opening easily again. However, if it's very warm weather, the window is likely to be swollen from the humidity. Wait for a dryer day. Then try this trick.

SAVING YOUR INSIDE WINDOW SILLS
If you have a lot of moisture build up on your windows, it can eventually damage your sills because of the water leakage. One way to improve this situation is to apply exterior housepaint to the sills. Be sure to refinish them, if necessary, before you paint them.

DON'T LET WOOD ROT COST YOU HEATING DOLLARS
Before the winter begins, take a tour of the exterior of your

home and look for wood rot around the windows. If you find it, be sure to remove rot and repair the areas. This is a prime spot for heat leakage so be sure to not let it slide.

KEEP YOUR SCREWS IN PLACE
If you've every been bothered by an annoying screw that keeps coming loose (and it can be especially dangerous in door knobs and other high activity locations) add a little nailpolish—or even a spot of glue—to the underside of the screw. Screw it into place and tape over for 24 hours. Gently remove tape and the screw should be firmly in place.

DON'T DAMAGE YOUR WALL WHEN YOU HAMMER
If you're afraid of "denting" your wall with unsightly hammer marks, protect your wall with a little foam rubber. Just place a piece over the nail head in the final stages of hammering. It will give you that extra bit of wall protection.

HANG PICTURES AND PROTECT YOUR WALLS
If you're nervous about plaster cracking or chipping, try this trick the next time you're hanging pictures. Mark the spot with an "X" of tape. Hammer the nail into the center of the "X". It will protect your walls in the same way this "X" principle protects large pieces of framed glass.

A SIMPLE TRICK FOR REMOVING WALLPAPER
If you're not prepared to rent a steamer, try this trick. Use 2 tbsp. of any dishwasher detergent and add to one gallon of water. Apply with a paint roller and allow to soak in for 30 minutes. Reapply just before peeling. The paper should come right off.

AN INEXPENSIVE WAY TO SOUNDPROOF WALLS
If you'd like a little extra sound protection, try applying accoustical ceiling tiles to the wall. Your kids will be able to "yip it up" in their rooms and it won't bother you (or the neighbors).

DON'T BANISH OLD COTTON SOCKS!
Instead, save them and use them for special cleaning tasks. For example, if you have chair rail and crown moldings, just running

the sock over the wood will remove dust build-up. Cotton socks with spray wax on them can be used for other wood surfaces to shine and polish.

MAKE YOUR WINDOWS SPARKLE
Make your windows—and all glass surfaces—sparkle with this little trick. Add two tablespoons of any liquid fabric softener to a quart of lukewarm water. For added convenience, apply from a spray bottle. Wipe and sparkle.

CAN'T MAKE A MAGNETIC SCREWDRIVER WORK?
Some people just can't get those little screws to stick, so here's an easy way to make your own "magnetic" device. Take an eight inch long piece of masking tape. Push the screw through it with the sticky side facing you. Now stick the ends of the tape to the handle of the screwdriver. Now screw it into the wall.

DON'T SMUDGE YOUR WALLS WHEN YOU DO "SHOPWORK"
When removing nails with a claw hammer, protect your walls from hammer marks by placing a small piece of styrofoam or wood between the hammerhead and the wall.

A SPECIAL TIP FOR PANELING, WALLPAPERING, & TILING
If you've ever been distressed to see that the wall or floor shows through between seams, here's a way to avoid that problem. First, you can try doing a better job at matching the seams. But often, you must leave a tiny bit of room for breathing, or expansion in hot weather, etc. So, after you've selected your materials, find some matching paint. Paint a stripe down the wall at equal intervals where the seams would be. When you paper or panel, what peeks through will match.

STORING WALLPAPER, PANEL, ETC.
Most people roll up the leftover paper and keep in in the bottom of a seldom-used closet. Instead, try tacking it up on a wall (such as the attic or other low traffic area). That way, your paper and paneling will fade at approximately the same rate as that which

has already been hung. Any future patching won't be nearly so noticeable.

INSPECT YOUR WALLS BEFORE PAPERING
There's nothing like being in the middle of papering or paneling to discover the real imperfections in your walls. Before you begin, examine them closely under a strong light (such as sunlight). Look for bumps and other distortions which would affect what you are doing. Then check out the walls for their "plumbness." You'll most likely find that they aren't as even as they look. If you use some matching paint to fill in the corners, if the wallpaper doesn't quite meet, it won't be such a disaster. (And you'll know what you are up against.)

HAVE YOU EVER CARPETED A WALL?
It used to be that every home had walls constructed of thick, very solid plaster, and as a result, there was very little problem with noise seepage. Today, unfortunately, for most people that is quite a different situation. If you have a problem with soundproofing, "paper" the walls with carpeting. It will go a long ways towards keeping the noise down.

AIRING OUT THE HOUSE
Avoid moisture build-up and internal environmental pollution by airing out the house each day. This can be done by leaving doors and/or windows open for a few minutes. Make sure, if at all possible, there is some cross ventilation.

NAIL "POP" FIX-IT METHOD
It's not at all unusual for nails to "pop" from the lumber into which they were hammered. If this happens to you, don't bother to try and re-hammer it, instead repair it. Just hammer a drywall nail above *and* below the one that has popped. Drive them in far enough that they are slightly recessed. Cover over indentations with a bit of spackle and dab up with paint. Pull out the old nail, fill in the hole with a little filler and cover the indentation in the same way.

ONE WAY ONLY
If you want to wash walls and ceilings with more ease and less

toil, wipe down surfaces in one direction only—not back and forth.

REACH INTO THOSE CORNERS
Along with washing walls in one direction only, you might also want to use one of the squeeze sponges on a stick. Use it only for this purpose. And when it's time to reach up into the corners by the ceiling, you'll have easy access.

REPAIR TORN WINDOW SHADES
Get some extra life out of old shades with a little simple handy work. Take the shade down and lay it out on a flat surface. Mend the tear with several coats of clear nail polish. Apply to both sides of the tear.

USE SEMI-GLOSS OR HI-GLOSS PAINT FOR CERTAIN JOBS
Because these paints can withstand more regular cleaning, you might want to consider them for high traffic areas like kitchen, playroom, windows and sills. The more readily they clean, the less likely you will have to re-paint.

CHOOSE YOUR CLEANING CLOTHS CAREFULLY
If you've ever dusted walls and ceiling (especially on flat paint) with an old rag and were dismayed with the results, consider carefully the cloth which you used. (Many of the new materials are scotchguarded and "dirt-proof" and do nothing more than drag it from place to place.) Use a good cotton terry cloth. Use it *only* for clean dusting. Do not spray any wax on it or other solutions. You'll like the results.

TWO BUCKETS CUT WORK EFFORTS
If you're washing down walls, ceilings or windows, try this simple trick. Use two buckets instead of one! Fill one with your cleaning solution and leave the other empty. As you dip the sponge or cloth into the solution, squeeze it out into the empty bucket. That way the dirt collects in the empty bucket, not in the clean solution.

DON'T OVERLOOK YOUR DOORS

People will wash down walls and ceilings, but overlook doors (and they get the most wear and tear). Put it in your list to wipe them down regularly and you'll have less long term maintenance.

LABEL YOUR CLEANING SOLUTIONS

When you mix up a solution with which you are especially pleased, label the bottle with the following information—what it is, what it's used for, and the ingredients (so you can make it again).

QUICK 'N EASY SCREEN REPAIR

The next time you've got a little hole in your screen, whip out some clear nail polish and "paint" it back together. Use several coats so there are no drip marks. If the hole is big enough to require a patch, use some old screening and glue it into place.

A SIMPLE TRICK FOR SAFE GLASS REMOVAL

If you're faced with removing a broken window, here's a safe way to avoid glass shards. Lightly "paint" the glass, on both sides, with some glue. Glue on some old newspaper or magazine pages. Then gently remove the putty around the edges. The glass will come out without scattering pieces around—or cutting you in the process.

FIX YOUR BROKEN WINDOW PANE

If you've ever found a chip or tiny hole in your window pane, don't despair. Fill it in with some clear nail polish and it will seal it up tight. Apply in several thin coats for best results.

KEEP MESS LEVEL DOWN WHEN PAINTING WALLS & CEILINGS

Don't donate a pair of old shoes to painting when you can so easily protect them with a pair of old socks. Just slip them over the shoes or sneakers and throw them away at the end of the job. The splatters will go with them.

WET WINDOWS IN WINTER

If your windows bleed with moisture in the winter (often this condition is bad enough to water damage the sills), turn on an electric heater fan, set on warm, to face the window. It should clear up the condensation.

STORM WINDOWS DO MORE THAN INSULATE

Besides save you a lot of money on loss of heat, you'll also find that a storm window will reduce the condensation level that occurs on your windows.

VENETIAN BLINDS LOOK BETTER WHEN THEY ARE CLEAN

You can lightly dust your venetians, but to really clean them takes a little extra power. Next time they are dirty, give them a shower with a little disinfectant in the water. They'll shine right up. If you really want to brighten them and they are color proof, add a little dishwasher detergent to the water and let them soak for 15 minutes.

REDUCE SUNFADE

If your home is exposed to a lot of sunshine, you're likely to find fabrics fading over a relatively short time. Instead of keeping the curtains drawn all the time, try adding a protective film over the glass. It's applied from the inside and goes a long ways towards reflecting back the sunlight, while keeping the room pretty cheery.

HOW TO HAVE MORE BEAUTIFUL WINDOWS

If you want to spend less time cleaning your windows, here's how. Invest in a professional squeegee. It should be stainless steel. Make sure it is a professional squeegee, not one you can buy in a supermarket or hardware store. Then covet it like a family heirloom. One of the secrets to cleaning is not only in having this particular type of squeegee, but making sure it doesn't get used for anything else but this purpose. You'll be surprised at how it cuts down on streaks and smears.

MORE TRICKS FOR WINDOWS

Although there are plenty of cleaning aids out on the market, one of the simplest and most inexpensive is simply to add 3 tablespoons of ammonia to a gallon of lukewarm water. Before you begin with the ammonia solution, wipe down the window gently with a clean sponge (used just for this purpose only) which has been dipped in a sudsy solution of dish detergent and water. Then take a second clean sponge, and go over the window with the ammonia solution. Use your squeegee to dry.

HARD WATER GOT YOU DOWN

If you live in an area where hard water is a problem, you might want to invest in some bottled water for cleaning purposes. That may seem crazy, but when you look at the clouds and streaks on your glass, it may sound like a good idea. Add ammonia or dish detergent and wipe down those mirrors, windows and other glass surfaces. You'll be pleased with the results.

A LADDER MAKES YOUR WORKLOAD LIGHTER

It may not sound very exciting, but a ladder can go a long ways towards cutting your household chores down—especially when it comes to working on walls, ceilings and windows. There are three things to think about before you make the choice. 1) Where will you store it? If it's not easily accessible, it's almost as good as not having it. So make room for it in a handy place. 2) Make it lightweight. If you need three people to haul it around, it's not much good, even if it is accessible. 3) Choose a practical size. Generally, a five-foot ladder is just about right. It's easy to move (not unwieldy). And it's not too tall or too short. Try it out before you buy it.

A PORTABLE CLEANING UNIT

One of the great complaints (and a secret to working less hard) is to cut down on the number of steps you take. When you clean, take the stuff with you. Don't walk back and forth (even if it's only a few steps). Try setting your cleaning materials up on a tray (not in a bucket where you have to keep pulling them in and out and are likely to spill in the process). Keep the tray on the same level at which you are working for the least amount of expended effort.

SOAP UP YOUR NAILS

If you want to drive a nail or screw more easily into the wall, push it into an old bar of soap before you begin to hammer. The soap will act as a lubricant and make the job a lot easier.

HOT NAILS

To keep walls from splitting when you hammer in nails, try this. First drop the nails into very hot water. Let stand for 15 seconds and remove. Now sink the nail.

HOT SCREWS, TOO!

If you've ever had a screw you just can't remove, pass a match over the end of your screwdriver. While the tip is still hot, remove the screw. It's as easy as 1-2-3.

ERASE BLACK MARKS FROM THE WALLS

You might never think to use an ordinary, clean pencil eraser to remove scuff marks and other dirt from baseboards and walls, but it really works.

GUM ERASERS WORK MIRACLES, TOO!

If you have any cotton fabric as wall covering and it gets scuffed or smeared, try a gum eraser. It can be purchased at all art supply stores and most 5 & 10¢ stores.

LEMONS MAKE THE HOUSE SMELL GOOD

The next time you're cleaning windows and other glass surfaces, squeeze a few lemons into the water. Then dry with a lint-free cloth and polish up with old, crumbled newspaper.

TREAT YOUR WALLS LIKE DELICATE WASHABLES

Because paint, wallcoverings, etc., can be so delicate when it comes to color loss, treat them like delicates. The next time you're cleaning, mix up a solution of water and your favorite delicate clothes soap. Follow the instructions on the bottle.

IF YOUR WALLS ARE DELICATE AND DIRTY...

Still treat them like your delicate washables, using your favorite delicate clothes soap, but add some ammonia to the solution. It provides an extra cutting edge for dirt. But, be sure and test an inconspicuous spot on the wall before you launch into a full scale cleaning campaign.

YOU AND YOUR LADDER
A readily accessible ladder is a must for efficient household cleaning when it comes to reaching those hard-to-get-at-places, but make sure you invest in a sturdy ladder (or throw out your old one and get a good one). Rickety ladders are a sure source of serious accidents.

HEAVY DUTY DROP CLOTHS
Another essential household cleaning aid for walls, ceilings, and windows, is the drop cloth. Not the cheap plastic ones or an old sheet or blanket which you can so easily slip on, but ones like the professionals use. It's great for painting walls, to clean them, etc. Just lay them out on the floor and clean up will be so much easier and faster.

THINK BEFORE YOU PANEL
If you're thinking about paneling a room, you'll probably have two choices—unfinished wood that has a more natural look and finished paneling that is smooth surfaced. Choose whichever you like best, but remember this about each. Unfinished paneling requires more careful maintenance. Finished paneling can usually be cleaned with just a very light dusting.

WASHING WALLPAPER
Although most manufacturers claim that wallpaper is washable, you might want to test it before you launch into a real cleaning campaign. There's nothing worse than washing down a wall only to find you shouldn't have. Generally speaking, the higher gloss the finish is on the paper, the more likely it is that you can successfully wash it down.

ANOTHER TIP FOR WASHING WALLPAPER
Be gentle in the washdown! Most people don't realize that the pattern can fade substantially with a little elbow grease. So be gentle—and like most other surfaces—wash in one direction only, not back and forth.

IF YOUR WALLPAPER ISN'T WASHABLE, TRY THIS
Some non-washable wallpapers can actually be dry-cleaned. Try using an upholstery cleaner, but check this out by spot testing AND by inquiring about the process from the retailer where you bought the paper.

START YOUR WORK AT THE BOTTOM UP
Although most people tend to think about cleaning walls, wood-working, etc. from the top down, it's a common (labor causing) mistake. Start at the bottom and work your way up. That way, when you dribble, if you don't catch them, they fall on CLEAN walls. Start at the top and dribble, and it runs down dirty walls—causing you more work.

DRY YOUR WALLS AFTER WASHING
This may seem like an unnecessary extra step, but dry walls attract less dirt in the air and less moisture on the wall is better for the plaster.

WASH YOUR CEILINGS LAST
Again, this may sound out of order. But just as you start at the bottom up with walls, any drips from ceilings will fall upon clean walls—a far easier task to quickly clean with no dirt smears.

REMOVING WALL SPOTS
If you're cleaning spots from a wall or ceiling and not cleaning the whole wall, then be sure to "whisk" the spot. You do this by lightly working the spotted area and blending into the surrounding area. This way you won't be left with an obvious mark.

PROTECT YOUR FLOORS FROM THE WALLS
An added way to protect your floors from paint splatters (besides drop cloths) and to tape down old newspapers where the floor meets the baseboard or wall. It will give you added protection when you're edging—and faster clean up, too.

GIVE YOUR WALLS AND CEILINGS A FACE LIFT BEFORE PAINTING
It's important to allow for a good cleaning before you begin to

paint. Dust first with a whiskbroom then a light cleaning with
mild detergent and water. Dry with a clean cloth. Wait 24 hours
and then paint.

SWITCH PLATES AND OUTLET COVERS NEED EXTRA CARE
Carefully remove them with a screwdriver and put all screws,
plates and covers in a plastic bag for protection and easy access
when you go to put them back on.

SAVE ON AMOUNT OF PAINT
When pouring paint into a tray, avoid the temptation to fill it
up. Instead, pour only a small amount into the deep end and
then roll the roller out over the clean end. Paint will apply more
evenly to walls and ceilings.

A TIP FOR SORTING LEFTOVER PAINT
When you've finished up those walls and ceilings, mark leftover
cans (or jars) with the color paint, the room(s) it was used in, and
whether it was for the ceiling or walls.

SAFETY TIP
If you use oil based paint to coat your walls and ceilings, throw
out the newspapers and drop cloths when you are finished. They
are a fire hazard if left around.

EDGING YOUR WALLS AND CEILINGS
Start with the edging first, before you do the major portion of
the walls and ceilings. Not only will it act as a color guide, but
you're likely to have less "finishing" with a brush.

SHAG CARPETING CAN BE MASKED!
An easy way to protect shag carpeting from paint smears when
you're tackling the baseboard portion of the painting job is to
tape down the edge of the shag carpeting with masking tape. It
will protect and also act as a straight edge.

MAKE PAINTING CLEAN UP EASIER
Here's a simple little hint for the next time you're painting walls

and ceilings: Instead of putting paint cans, tray and other materials directly on a drop cloth, place them on newspaper on top of the drop cloth. That way you reduce the risk of accidentally getting wet paint on the floor, or other areas that take extra time to clean up.

TAPING WHEN YOU PAINT
Lots of people use masking tape or other tape to assist with straight edges and to protect certain areas when painting. Tape is helpful but here's an extra hint: Pre-test the surface by applying some tape, and if possible allowing it to remain on 24 hours. Use an inconspicuous area so that if by any chance the tape removes the paint, you won't be saddled with an extra repair.

READ THE INSTRUCTIONS ON YOUR PAINT CAN!
Who ever thought there would be instructions on a paint can, but often there are. If it's homogenized paint, do not stir—and the instructions on the paint can will so inform you. Stirring homogenized paint can cause air bubbles.

MISCELLANEOUS
(fireplace, books, drawers, records, tools, metals, etc.)

INTRODUCTION FOR MISCELLANEOUS

Any household, from the smallest apartment to the largest home, requires a lot of care and good maintenance to not only keep things looking nice but to also help insure longer service. In this chapter we've rounded up all of the items which don't fall under the usual areas of kitchen, floors, furniture, laundry, etc. and given you one of the best chapters we've seen on miscellaneous items.

We help you get rid of sink odors and clean drains. We tell you how to keep jewelry, records, leather-bound books and ball point pens in good condition. We give you tips on removing bumper stickers and how to make your own eyeglasses cleaner—all the extra small tips that make your life easier and more pleasant. This brief but handy guide will help you clean and preserve not only all your household belongings, but your outdoor supplies as well.

WHAT TO DO WITH MESSY BARBEQUE GRILLS:
First of all, to avoid the mess coat your grill with a lot of vegetable oil before cooking. This will eliminate the need to deal with burnt on grease afterward. But, if you are already trying to cope with the after effects of a cookout, simply wrap the grill in a piece of heavy duty aluminum foil, dull side up. Heat the charcoal to a very high degree and then place the grill over the coals for approximately 10 or 12 minutes. When you remove the foil, all the burnt on grease and food drippings will fall off and your grill will look as clean as when you purchased it.

HOW CAN I CLEAN THE INSIDE OF MY STEAM IRON?
It's easy. Just fill the iron with an equal amount of water and white vinegar and let it steam for about five minutes. Then turn it off and allow to stand for about an hour. When you empty the iron and rinse with clean water, all the collected mineral deposits should disappear.

HOW CAN I CLEAN THE BROWN SPOTS FROM THE BOTTOM OF MY STEAM IRON?

To avoid staining clothes with the burnt-on spots that collect on the bottom of any iron with time, simply mix a solution of vinegar and salt and heat it up. Then use this to clean the outside of the iron. The spots should come off easily.

HERE'S A HOMEMADE SOLUTION FOR EYEGLASS CLEANER.

Just use an eyedropper of vinegar (or vodka if you have any) on each lens, and wipe clean. Your lenses will be bright and have no streaks.

BUT, WHAT ABOUT *REALLY* DIRTY SCREENS?

Well, I can't imagine that anything could be *that* dirty, but here goes. Try removing the screens from the doors and using a mixture of steaming, hot water, ammonia and your outdoor hose. Scrub them down with a soft sponge, and the hot water and ammonia and then let rip with the spray attachment of your hose. That'll show the dirt who's boss!

EVERYONE HATES TO CLEAN VENETIAN BLINDS.

So, with that in mind, here is the most painless way to go about it. Simply take down the blinds and hang them out on your clothesline. Next, take a big, soft sponge and attach it to the end of a ruler or yardstick. Use this "device" to scrub down the blinds with detergent and hot water. Then, get the garden hose and rinse all that dirt away.

BUT, WHAT ABOUT SMALL SPOTS ON MY BLINDS? DO I HAVE TO GO THROUGH ALL THAT?

No, certainly not. For small spots and marks (touch-up work, really) just go to the local art supply store and get yourself an art gum eraser. Now, just "erase" those smudges.

BUT WHAT ABOUT SIMPLE DUSTING?

The easiest way to avoid cuts and scrapes while dusting venetian blinds is to cover your hand with an old sock. Makes a great dusting mitt!

ARE YOUR ARTIFICIAL FLOWERS LOOKING OLD AND SOILED?

Put the flowers in a large paper bag and add some salt. Seal the bag and shake vigorously. The salt will remove dust and soil from your flower and they'll look as good as new.

EVER WONDER HOW TO CLEAN A BALL POINT PEN?

Simply insert the point into the filter portion of a cigarette and turn a few times. This will remove excessive ink and fuzz from the pen point.

WANT TO REFURBISH YOUR CANDLES BEFORE DINNER TONIGHT?

To make candles look clean and shiny like new, just wipe them off with a piece of cotton dipped in rubbing alcohol.

MESSY WAX BUILD UP ON YOUR SILVER CANDLE HOLDERS?

Try these two easy methods: 1) Place the holders in the freezer for about an hour, and then remove. The wax should peel off easily. 2) Or if you prefer, simply run hot water over the candle holders and let the wax fall off. Wipe dry with a paper towel.

DO YOUR CANVAS AWNINGS REMIND YOU OF A BIRD SANCTUARY?

To clean them off, use a stiff brush that you have run over a bar of naphtha soap and then dusted with dry washing soda. Follow with a good hosing.

CIGARETTE SMOKE CAN BE *CLEANED* FROM THE AIR.

All you have to do is soak a towel in water and wring it out well. Then briskly swing it around. The towel will collect the smoke.

WANT TO CLEAN YOUR CRYSTAL CHANDELIER WITHOUT DISMANTLING IT?

Simply wear a pair of cotton work gloves and dip your fingers in ammonia water. Use your fingers to clean the chandelier.

HOW ABOUT A LESS-WORK WAY TO WASH AND MAINTAIN YOUR CAR?

Forget the old soap and water routine. Instead, try washing your jalopie with a bucket of hot water that's had a cup of kerosene added to it. Wipe the car down with this mixture and then rinse. Wipe dry with soft, clean cloths. No need to wax, you'll see water bead up and run off.

HERE'S A TIP ON HOW TO GET THOSE OLD BUMPER STICKERS OFF.

A little lighter fluid will do the trick. Soak the stickers down good, and when they become saturated, use a single edge razor blade to ease them off your bumper.

THOSE YECH-Y SPLATTERED BUGS CAN BE CLEANED OFF EASILY.

A little good, old baking soda and an old net bag (like the kind you buy potatoes in) will do the trick.

GOT TAR ON YOUR RUG MATS? HERE'S A WAY TO CLEAN THAT PROBLEM UP IN A HURRY.

Soak the ugly tar spots in a generous dose of linseed oil. Let it soak for about 15 minutes, and blot it up with a dampened cloth. Wash your mats as usual afterward.

DO I NEED TO SCRUB THE FIREPLACE FLOOR?

No. To reduce soot just threw salt on the logs from time to time.

REMOVING OIL FROM GARAGE FLOORS.

If the garage floor is made of concrete, you can remove oil spills and drippings by soaking the spot with mineral spirits for about one-half hour and then scrubbing with a hard brush and more mineral spirits. Follow the scrubbing with a layer of newspaper to absorb the oil and moisture. Then let the concrete dry. When it is dry, clean the area with solution of laundry detergent mixed with 1 cup of bleach in 1 gallon of cold water. Repeat process if necessary.

AN INEXPENSIVE WAY TO CLEAN OLD JEWELRY:

Just dip a soft cloth in toothpaste and wipe jewelry clean.

TWO NATURAL AND EFFICIENT WAYS TO CLEAN PEWTER VESSELS:

To clean pewter vessels either rub with cabbage leaves or if you prefer, use a mixture wood ashes and water (only a small amount to moisten). Pewter will clean up quickly.

HOW TO CLEAN THE DIRT AND DUST FROM BETWEEN THE BUTTONS OF YOUR TELEPHONE:

Take a Q-tip dipped in rubbing alcohol and wipe between the spaces. Then use a cloth dampened in the alcohol to clean the rest of the phone. It should look as shiny as new.

HOW CAN I GET RID OF THOSE UGLY STAINS IN THE BOTTOM OF MY VASES?

To clean the inside of vases, especially those with openings too small for your hand to fit in, just moisten the inside of the vase with a little water and then add a little toilet bowl cleaner. After about 10 minutes the stains will be removed.

EVEN CLEAN CARPET CAN SOMETIMES LOOK OLD AND GRUNGY.

However, here's a quick tip to "cheer" up your faded carpet's glory. Just take a medium sized box of cornstarch and toss it liberally over your carpet. Let it stand at least an hour. Vacuum it up, and your carpet will look fresh as new.

MUD SPOTS ARE THE REAL ENEMY OF SPOTLESS CARPETS.

And cornstarch can be your friend here, too. As long as the mud stains are still damp, cover them with a liberal helping of cornstarch and wait about a half hour. Once the cornstarch has soaked up all the yech-y mud, vacuum the stain away.

WHAT ABOUT DIRTY FOOTPRINTS?

Well, on light colored carpets, try a gum eraser!

BUT, WHAT ABOUT *REALLY* DIRTY FOOTPRINTS?

Again, pour a generous helping of salt on the dirty mark and let it stand for a half an hour or so. Then, vacuum the dirt away.

AND INK MARKS ON YOUR CARPET SHOULD BE HANDLED THE SAME WAY AS ON YOUR CLOTHES.
Spray the mark with hairspray and let it dry. After a few minutes, blot the stain away with a cloth dampened in a three to one solution of water and white vinegar.

CLEANING PLASTIC TABLES AND CHAIRS CAN LEAVE THEM WITH A BAD CASE OF THE SMEARS.
Plastic furniture can really look smeared after you've cleaned it. Just put a little lemon oil on a clean, cotton rag and wipe those smears right out of your life.

NOW THAT YOU'VE CLEANED OUT THE SINK, HAVE YOU CLEANED OUT THE ODORS, TOO.
Don't just clean your sink, clean your drain, too, or the kitchen sink isn't really clean. Pour a cup of regular household bleach down the drain. Let it sit for a few minutes and then flush for five to seven minutes with running water. Bleach left standing in the drain could corrode it.

CLEANING TIPS FOR THE FIREPLACE.
When its time to clean out the fireplace, here's a handy tip to remember. Before shoveling out the ashes in your fireplace for your annual Spring cleaning (or just because they've gotten so high that you no longer get any wood in!) remember to use your plant spritzer to wet down the ashes. That way, they won't fly all over the room when you shovel them out.

ASHES TO ASHES...
Actually, those dirty ashes have a very real and useful purpose; you can use them to *easily* clean your fireplace doors or glass screens. Just put some of the ashes on a damp cloth and rub them (in a circular motion) into the dirty glass. Rinse with clear, warm water and another damp rag, and they'll be clean.

MORE ON ASHES (OR, IN THIS CASE, ASHTRAYS)...
Ceramic ashtrays can really "hold" onto ground in cigarette and cigar ashe. Consequently, here's a cleaning tip that'll cut your ashtray cleaning time down to a fraction. Just take some of your

favorite furniture or floor polish and a clean rag and polish the inside of the ashtray. It'll wipe clean in seconds!

EVER WONDER HOW TO CLEAN THE TARNISH OUT FROM BETWEEN THE PRONGS OF YOUR SILVER FORKS?

Well, wonder no more! Just dip an ordinary pipe cleaner in silver polish and clean away.

HERE ARE SOME TIPS FOR CLEANING SCREENS.

Use the dusting attachment of your vacuum cleaner to "dust" those hard to clean screens clean.

If your screens are really dirty, remove them and try this. With a clean paint brush, "paint" kerosene onto both sides of the screen. Let it dry, and then rinse it with warm water. After rinsing, wash with soap and water and rinse again. Voila! Clean screens.

ARE YOUR STAINLESS STEEL POTS, AND PANS AND UTENSILS OLD AND UGLY LOOKING?

Well, clean and brighten them up with a thinly applied coat of over cleaner, and then rinse them *very* thoroughly.

A MULTITUDE OF TIPS FOR WASHING THE CAR.

Did you know that good old coca-cola and a little aluminum foil can clean rust off your car bumpers?

HOW ABOUT WHITE-WALL TIRES?

Simple. Just use one of those steel wool pads with soap already in it and a little hot water.

BUT, (YOU'RE PROBABLY WONDERING) HOW DO I CLEAN UNDER THE CAR?

Rust can work it's way anywhere on your car, but the underside is particularly vulnerable. Corrosive road salts can easily eat away a spot that will soon turn to rust. However, you can wash the underside of your car with little effort and no trouble. Just set the sprinkler under the car and turn it on. Move it occasionally so that the entire under-belly gets washed.

EVEN WINDSHIELD WIPERS GET DIRTY.

And, when they do, they'll streak up your windshield and restrict visability. But, they can easily be cleaned. Just wash them down with hardy solution of baking soda and warm water.

HOW TO GET RID OF STREAKS.

Simple. Just wash your car in the shade, and you'll alleviate all streaking.

TAKE A CLOSE LOOK AT YOUR BOOK SHELVES SOMETIME.

Bookshelves and books make a perfect trap for dirt and dust in your home, and it's so easy to take them for granted and let them alone. However, take a good look at them (in your own house) sometime.

I know, I know; dusting all those books is time consuming and very, *very* boring. But, bear with me. Simply arrange your books so that they are at the front of the shelves, to allow air circulation and prevent trapping of moisture that would promote mildew. The next time you vacuum, simply use the attachment for furniture and/or crevices and vacuum your books clean!

IF YOU HAVE OLD, ANTIQUE, LEATHER-BOUND BOOKS, HERE'S A TIP FOR YOU.

From time to time, do more than just vacuum them. You see, the air will dry out leather-bound books, causing them to crack and crumble. So, oil them occasionally, with a light furniture or leather oil.

YOUR DRAINS GET DIRTY, TOO.

Especially the kitchen drain. All the greasy bits and pieces of food that disappear down it, even if you're careful, are bound to clog it eventually. So, from time to time, clean it out, by pouring a large pan of boiling water down it. Follow it up by a heavy dose of your favorite liquid cleanser and lemon juice (to freshen it), and then rinse it again with boiling water. The drain will run faster, and smell a whole lot cleaner, too.

CLEANING UP PAINT BRUSHES CAN BE A SNAP!

For instance, if you are cleaning out your brush after shellacking something, do this: dip the brush into denatured alcohol first, and then brush it vigorously back and forth across a newspaper. Do this several times, and then wash the brush with a regular detergent and water combination. Your brush will be completely clean.

MORE ABOUT CLEANING YOUR PAINT BRUSHES...

It makes a difference as to how you clean your brushes depending on the type of paint you've been painting with. For instance, clean up your brush after using latex paint (which is water soluble) by first "working" the brush with your hands under warm, running water. Next, wash the bristles with a detergent and water combo.

If you have been painting with an oil-based paint, you should first clean out the excess paint in a jar of paint thinner or turpentine (if you plan on letting the brush soak, make sure that the amount of thinner in the can or jar *just* covers the bristles and no more). Then, wash the brush with a detergent under warm, running water.

AND, THERE'S AN IMPORTANT STEP AFTER WASHING.

After washing your brushes thoroughly, go outside and shake them vigorously before putting them away.

AND HERE'S A TIP ON HOW TO KEEP THOSE BRUSHES CLEAN AFTER YOU'VE WASHED THEM.

Store the paint brushes (if they are going to be used again soon) wrapped in plastic wrap, the type you use in your kitchen. If you won't be using them again for a while, wrap them tightly in brown paper, but always make sure they are thoroughly dry first, or they may mildew.

IF SOMEONE HAS PUT A BRUSH AWAY DIRTY, DON'T THROW IT AWAY. THERE'S STILL A WAY TO CLEAN IT.

Take the dirty brush and gently "comb" the bristles with a stiff wire brush.

ONE LAST TIP ABOUT CLEANING UP AFTER PAINTING...

Remember that most paint rollers are reusable, too. They should be cleaned the same way you would clean your paint brushes; according to the type of paint you were using in it.

INK ON YOUR WOODWORK, SHAME ON YOU!

Shame on you, because here's a quick tip on how to remove it. Take a clean cotton cloth and a bottle of distilled white wine vinegar. Using the vinegar straight from the bottle, lightly blot at the offensive marks. Keep blotting until they disappear.

THE EXHAUST OVER YOUR STOVE IS A "HOT-BED" OF GREASE AND DIRT.

Of course you know, as well as anyone, that greasy, yucky dirt is lurking inside the cover to your kitchen exhaust fan, but no one wants to scrape and scrub to get it clean. So, here's the easier, and more efficient, solution, just put the fan and the grating in the dishwasher and let the machine do the dirty work.

THOSE ANTIQUE, INTRICATELY PLEATED LAMP-SHADES CAN REALLY BE *!?#! TO CLEAN.

But, here's the solution. Just use your electric hairdryer to blow out all the dust and dirt from the crevices and those intricate pleats.

CLEANING YOUR MICRO-WAVE OVEN IS A CINCH.

Just use your plant mister to dampen the inside of the oven. Then turn the oven on high for about seven seconds. Let the oven cool down and you can wipe it clean in a jiffy.

WHAT ABOUT CAR WINDOWS?

Cleaning glass can often be a frustrating experience, because it streaks so easily. However, the next time you wash your car windows, after washing rub them down with newspaper and all the streaks will be gone.

VINYL SEATS ARE A SNAP TO CLEAN.

Use a clean, damp cloth and a liquid, self-stripping floor wax and your seats will clean up like new in no time. And your floor mats can be dropped into the washing machine with some old rags and towels.

ORGANIZATION IS IMPORTANT.
As in housework, so in car washing! Have one bucket of soapy water to wash with, and one bucket of clear water to rinse with. Use three or four towels or rags. One to wash with , one to rinse with, and one or two to dry with. You'll find it much easier and you won't have as many towels to wash afterward!

AUTO GREASE NEED NOT BE A CLEAN-UP PROBLEM.
It can easily be cleaned up with ordinary baking soda and warm water.

OIL DRIPS ON YOUR GARAGE FLOOR NEED NOT BE A PROBLEM TO CLEAN UP.
Just spread a little kitty litter over the grease stain, let it sit and then sweep those stains away.

RECORDS ARE CLEANABLE, TOO.
Of course, that doesn't mean you should throw them in the washing machine. *However, they can be cleaned.* When cleaning or washing records, the most important thing to remember is to rub the record in a circular motion, moving with the grooves of the record, *never against them.*

DO YOU HATE CLEANING THE SINKS IN THE BATHROOM AND KITCHEN BECAUSE IT'S SO HARD TO GET AROUND THE FAUCETS AND THE NOOKS AND CRANNIES.
Well, everyone else hates it, too. But, it's got to be done. So, just use an old toothbrush to get at all those annoying little areas.

GET RID OF SOAP DISH GUNK!
Just cut a small sponge in two and place it under the soap on the soap dish, and presto!, no more soap "gunk"!

CLEANING TIPS FOR OIL PAINTINGS.

Never rub an oil painting with a dusting cloth. Instead, use an ultra soft sable hair paint brush to lightly dust the picture clean.

CLEANING THE WALL BEHIND THE STOVE CAN BE A REAL PAIN.

But, it doesn't have to be. "Polish" the area behind the stove with a healthy coating of your favorite furniture polish. Ten, the next time you go to clean the greasy dirt off the wall, you'll find it wipes back off.

WANT TO AVOID TAKING YOUR DIAMOND TO THE JEWELER TO HAVE IT CLEANED?

All you have to do to clean a diamond is place it in a wire strainer and dip for a few seconds into a solution of boiling water, soap flakes and ammonia. Let the diamond cool before rinsing, and then soak in a bowl of alcohol for about 10 minutes. It can be dried with a piece of tissue.

PICTURE FRAMES CAN BE CLEANED TO LOOK LIKE NEW.

Moisten a sponge with a small amount of turpentine and wipe all around the frame. Let the frame dry for one or two days before touching.

RUSH CAN BE QUICKLY AND EASILY CLEANED FROM LAWN AND GARDEN TOOLS.

Use a soapy steel-wool pad dipped in either kerosene or turpentine and wash the tools. Follow with a brisk application of aluminum foil wadded up into a ball. All of the rust should lift off the tools and they should resume their shine.

DON'T YOU HATE TO CLEAN THE FIREPLACE?

Well, you can cut down on the amount of cleaning you have to do by throwing some regular table salt on the logs and it'll cut down on the amount of soot and consequently, on the amount of clean-up you have to do.

CONCLUSION

All of the hints in this book are designed to make your life simpler by cutting down the amount of time you need to spend on your house. Many of them also save you money, because they're geared to give you not only the best, but the most economical way to do a task. We hope that with all the time you'll save by using the tips that there is plenty of extra time to do all of the things that please you the most!!